ATTRACTIVE
UNATTRACTIVE
AMERICANS

HOW THE WORLD SEES AMERICA

RENÉ ZOGRAFOS

Renessanse publishing 2015

renezografos.com

ISBN 978-82-998598-8-2

Content editing and proofreading: Lauren Hidden

Book design and cover: Damonza.com

Attractiveunattractiveamericans.com

This book is dedicated to all who have travelled to America to build a country of individual freedom, fairness and faith. This book is for all Americans who haven't given up on their country, and for making America a little bit better every day.

To dreamers, lovers, entrepreneurs, equal rights- and freedom fighters, outsiders, new thinkers and fighters for peace and kindness on our globe – this world would be poor without you – Thank you!

Thanks to all the people around the world who have participated with their observations and thoughts to this book - it was an honor to meet you all!

"The land of the free and the home of the brave!" That's how this book had to start because I believe that these specific words from the American national anthem are still significant for every single American. I have no doubt in my mind that Americans value their freedom. In almost every aspect of the American way of life, people from other countries can see and experience the freedom to speak, the freedom to defend themselves, the freedom to be who they are. The braveness goes back a long time—from the first people who came to the Wild West to all the people who live in America now. No other nation has such a short and valiant history as America. No other nation is comparable, and no other country is as famous as America. Almost every adult human being on the globe knows something, and even feels something, about America. But what do they really know about this great country? More important, what does the rest of the world think about the average American? What is the naked truth when it comes to America and the people who live there?

With these questions in mind I started the journey of writing this book. I traveled around the world to ask people what there is to like and dislike about America.

People outside of America have an ideal picture about the American lifestyle; many people, especially those who haven't been there, have a very romantic view of the country. People have experienced the magical stories produced by Hollywood. Countless numbers of people in the world have their own American hero—perhaps a great musician, a leading actor or actress in a film, a great athlete, or a famous author. We have seen the breathtaking scenery between the West and the East Coast. And we have tasted American food and drinks like hamburgers and Coca-Cola.

Americans are also known for doing memorable things.

They like to build the tallest buildings. They sent the first person to the moon. The fastest man on earth is almost always an American, and they also like to be innovative. To be the first, the best and the wisest is fundamental in America.

But still, what does a world that contains seven billion people think about a great nation like America? To ask every single person in the world is, of course, an impossible task! Therefore, I have gathered honest opinions from people in countries in each and every continent on the globe. I traveled from the coldest to the warmest places and met rich and poor. I documented both very negative and very positive opinions. I encountered dreamers and realists, and professionals and intellectuals. Most important, I met random people from all parts of the world, and they all had one thing in common; they wanted to tell the truth about what they thought of the land of the free and the home of the brave.

So America, this is how the rest of the world sees you!

René Zografos

TABLE OF CONTENTS

American Rawness 1

Mother Earth 4

"In Sweden, We Have a System..." 6

American Girls Under Pressure 10

"Working 9 to 5"?. 11

Frank Leslie Rix 13

Many Seem to Have a Love and Hate Relationship with America. 18

Five People in Oslo, Norway. 21

America, the New Empire 23

Eight Americans about America 25

A Fashion Report from the UK. 27

Three on a Cruise Ship in the Mediterranean Ocean 30

Up from Down Under 31

Five Random People in Stockholm, Sweden 33

Spoiled American Kids 34

The World vs. the USA. 36

American Explorers. 39

Surf's Up 43

Three on Fuerteventura, a Spanish Island 45

The Remote American Dream. 46

Evan about American Beer 49

Evan about Drinking 50

Five People in Nice, France. 51

From a Stylist's View. 52

Observations from a Vagabond 54

How to Achieve Success in America 56

American Sports 56

American Music 58

About the USA 62

The American Dream 63

Four in Egypt 65

My First Day in "Big" America 67

Eight from England about America 72

Greetings from Canada 74

Fat and Fatter 75

Cuban Food-Libré 76

Deadly American Advice 78

A Foreigner in America 84

From the Downton Abbey 87

About Lack of Discipline: 87

About Moving to Britain: 87

Maestro 88

Three people in Dubai, United Arab Emirates 89

The United States of America 90

Six from the Cradle of Western Civilization 94

At the Therapist's Office 96

Ship Ahoy! 102

Mother, Mother 104

Pelekas News 106

Five Americans on Manhattan, New York 108

Five Foreigners on Manhattan, New York 110

Thank You 111

Americans in Mexico 112

Five Random People in Madrid, Spain 113

Happy Holidays 114

The Law of Jante 118

The Law of Jante: 121

The New Law 121

Moods from the Sahara Desert 125

The Economic Wind. 127

The top 25 most prosperous nations in the world: 129

From the Fairway 131

Woof Woof. 133

What I Have Learned from Americans 135

The Jailhouse Blues Pages 139

On and Off in the USA 143

Bringing Disgrace upon Their Country. 145

The America I Knew. 146

Dear Brother 148

Three Random People from Germany. 159

Words of Wisdom. 160

On a Remote Island in the Indian Ocean 163

Five in Florence, Italy 165

At the Dentist's Office. 166

Summary 168

Is the American Dream Still Reachable? 171

Handicrafts and the Workforce. 173

Time off. 176

TV problems 177

How We Want our Americans to Be 181

Positive Attention, Please 185

American Eating Habits 189

American Efficiency 192

The Real Wild West 194

"Happy Land" 199

American Pop Culture 202

Old America. 207

Young Americans 210

Attractive, Unattractive Americans 213

An American is Not Really a Stereotypical American. 216

The Dead American Countryside 219

Carpe Diem 221

AMERICAN RAWNESS

AMERICANS WANT TO win. Good is not good enough for an American. They don't even know what "good" is. Not even "Best-in-class" at work, or ranked nationally, is good enough for an American; they don't have limits for excellence. To be the best in the world is all that matters to Americans. When I search for job candidates, I always seek the best people in the world in their area of expertise, and I almost always end up with an American.

The Americans have an extreme "winner" mentality, and that's what is needed to achieve success. They never lose sight of their goals, and the work they have to carry out is just another border they must cross. Americans don't look back, because they have their goal in sight; they don't listen to others who say they can't make it. And their self-esteem grows as they get stronger and better at the tasks that will help them reach their goal. Anyone who tries to be the best can tell you that there are a lot of temptations and distractions along the way, but Americans seem to be good at avoiding them and accepting that changes in life will influence them. They are good at sharing their dreams with others. They talk freely about them, and tell people how they plan to achieve their specific dreams. They also envision their dreams every day until they have reached the finish line.

The Americans' spirit of competition starts at school. It is normal and acceptable for students to compete in American schools, and that is the opposite from where I come from, as well as for the rest of Europe, where competition has a negative connotation.

Americans also listen when another person gives them advice.

In Europe, that is rare; we don't easily take advice from others. Even when the person giving the advice is an expert in their field, we do not easily follow their words. This separates us from Americans who are eager to try new things and to share experiences and advice.

Author Jim Collins once said, "Good is the enemy of great." I find that expression to be true for the American people. If an American man has earned ten million dollars, he will soon make one hundred million because he has big goals. Some people might call those who make ten million dollars lucky, but, in my opinion, Americans make their own luck because they are focused on their goals and have a clear vision of what it takes to achieve them. An American will never be satisfied in second or third place because there is a higher goal to achieve—first place. So, the reason why an American can't be satisfied with making ten million dollars is because the possibility of making one hundred million is ever- present.

There is no doubt that hard work beats talent, and Americans understand this principle. They put in the hard work, step by step and systematically. They walk the talk and they win in the end.

In a competitive situation, Americans have a rawness about their approach. They show no fear and they maintain focus. Look at the Williams sisters of the tennis world, Serena and Venus; if their main focus would be on the scoreboard instead of their tennis technique, they would not succeed. Americans manage to focus on the simple and important things that matter, and that's why the best athletes in the world are found in America.

The best American athletes also have a crazy mindset that leads them to believe it is necessary to be a superstar. They like to put other competitors down, to psyche them out and act as if they are superheroes.

In my opinion, Americans are lucky to have such a winning mentality ingrained in their culture. They have a way of focusing on only the positive things when it comes to achieving their goals. They truly believe in the American dream, and their family stands behind them all the way to the finish line.

Cecilie Ystenes is a certified consultant and business coach in Europe and USA. Her clients come from a variety of businesses and top international sporting leagues such as: Premier League football (soccer) clubs, and the American police force. She also works as a consultant through Lee Hecht Harrison in the United States of America.

"Before I went to America I was a shy little student afraid of almost everything in this world, but America taught me to be brave and outgoing. Thank you, America."

Sandra, Germany

"An American speaks to us as [if] we ought to know everything about his country. If we did the same to an American, that person would be very, very lost."

Stephanie, Luxembourg

MOTHER EARTH

BEFORE, IT WAS understandable that Americans were always thinking in big terms. Now, I feel that the American way of thinking has to change. America is a very new country when compared to the rest of the world. The first American settlers had enormous space for themselves. Therefore, the roads they built were wide, and the cars also had to be big to fit the roads. They built their houses big because they could, and then they needed a big refrigerator in the house to fill the space. This 'bigger is better' trend just continued. In other places, like Asia and Europe, they learned to live simpler. In my opinion, Americans have lived long enough without thinking about Mother Earth. Americans spend frivolously and throw away things more quickly than anyone else. The consumerism is way above the average of that of any other world citizen and grows capitalism further and further. Americans need to wake up from their own little world!

Gisele, from Paris, France

"Think of all the fine, hardworking people who were the first travelers to America—the people who built the country. I sense that they would be very disappointed if they could see what condition their country is in now."

Sandra, Estonia

Did you know?

It is forbidden to build a house with less than five thousand square feet in Beverly Park in Los Angeles.

"IN SWEDEN, WE HAVE A SYSTEM..."

T HE SWEDISH ARE known for their attitude; we think we have something to teach to the rest of the world. Even here in little Sweden, one can often find preconceived comments about how bad everything is outside of our borders. America is the country we want to talk about most when we share opinions on how things should be done.

In the most recent presidential election in 2012, Sweden expressed more statements than usual about how crazy Americans are and that they lack the sanity to vote as honorable Swedish people would. Not infrequently, Swedish people make statements about the Swedish welfare state, equality and the excellences of their equality state. But the self-satisfaction of the Swedish ought to make every human being sick if they have a trifle of objectivity in their body. The stuck-up comments from Swedes stem from something that reminds them of an unhappy love story. We love, admire and constantly crave to be like Americans, but they do not return our adoration. Americans mix us up with some other country that begins with an S, "Swiweden or what was the name again?"

As if that wasn't enough, humiliated, we realize that our great love for America is worn on our sleeve, obvious to all, including ourselves and Americans. Americans manage to take care of themselves without our good Swedish advice, benevolence and attention. No other country has as many Nobel Prize winners as the United States. The latest technology, medicine, movies, music and everything we perceive as "the newest" comes from America. Of course, it can be noted that American hegemony sometimes is disturbed by up-and-coming countries, like China, who impress us with their ambitions toward labor, growth and economic stability. However, it is clear that countries like China look to one specific country as their primary inspiration—America.

The current economic crises and the low conjuncture also injure the USA's highly esteemed reputation. That worries us; it concerns us when the one who we have all hope for doesn't live up to our expectations. But this worry also gives us a reason, to again, tell Americans about Sweden and how we think things should be done. We are proud to showcase how good our country is financially, and we like to point out that *The Financial Times* selected our Swedish finance minister as the "Finance Minster of the Year, 2012." That is a major award!

So, in our comments and greetings to the country "over there," we Swedes explain willingly how we believe the USA should have done things. Of course, we believe they should strive to be more like us: raise taxes, secularize the religious population and, as soon as possible, build the same welfare state that Sweden did in the 1970s. And for God's sake, let wealth be synonymous with "stealing from the poor." Only then could the United States be more easily understood, and more important, America would be much better because they would be more Swedish.

Perhaps our love story goes back longer than we believe—to a time long before America gave us rock music, movie stars, dreams and the iMac. Wasn't it our close family members who once left the captive and poor lands of Europe to build anew and big in the

West? Why should those who left to escape religious oppression, tax collectors, counts, barons, emperors and kings ever expose themselves to that again? Why build a copy of Europe when you could build a better country in America with freedom of expression, economic liberty and religious independence of the United States? It stings a bit for the Scandinavians to acknowledge that the people who left did it to start something new.

Let it also be said that there are those who believe that everything in the U.S. is good, but some people argue that Americans in general are a trigger-happy, overweight population that believes in God but not in the welfare state. Therefore, this disparity of opinion creates a natural need to provide an alternative picture. However, neither image is correct. The U.S. is perhaps like most people: both good and bad.

You cannot paint a picture of America and get a homogeneous portrait of the country. It is broader and more diverse than what can be written in the chronicles and analyses. But America is fascinating and it is the country that, more than any other, gives us hope. We always glance westward to seek ideas and solutions. A humble view is that we have more to learn from the U.S. than they do of us.

Maria Ludvigsson is an award-winning columnist writer in the Swedish newspaper,

Svenska Dagbladet.

"It's Americans' fault that I don't have any money left! Everything had to be so damn cheap over there that it was impossible to not buy everything I like."

Linn, Norway

"In America you are, in fact, not considered weird if you talk to people you just have met on the street; it's the opposite [reaction] where I come from"

Theresa, Hungary

AMERICAN GIRLS UNDER PRESSURE

66 ALL THE GIRLS who struggle to be the prettiest ones in America must go through fire, in my opinion. It must be very hard for them to live up to the pressure. And the fact that they have so many "Miss" contests on all levels, from birth to mature adult, to confirm that they are the pretty and the special one, makes it even harder for them. Having many different beauty contests also means that there are many winners, so it's not really as special to win one. So when a woman finally wins a contest, she also discovers that almost everyone else has won one at some point or another. So the [beauty] goals must be even higher now, in modern days, because an American must "stand out" and be way more special than the girl next door. She can't settle down to be Miss Idaho when her friend becomes Miss USA—now she must strive to be Miss Universe. The nightmares of competition seem to continue forever for these girls."

Magda, New Zealand

"I think Americans are brainwashed, but, then again, too brainwashed to understand that they are."

Luis, Paraguay

"WORKING 9 TO 5"?

"Americans work twice as much as we do in Europe, but we earn twice as much as they do in the States."

Olivier, Belgium

"Americans must certainly learn to slow down! Even on vacation they are very stressed. If Americans, for some reason, don't bring their work with them when they are on holiday, they must do something else to be active. Relaxation never seems to be an option. They come across as very stressed to me, so they must learn to relax."

Maria, Chile

DID YOU KNOW?

U.S. workers put in more hours on their job than the labor force of any other industrial nation. Japan held the record for most hours on   the job until around 1995, but Americans now work almost *a month more than the Japanese and three months more than Germans, annually. Americans are also working harder. Nearly 40% of workers described their office environment as, "like a real life Survivor program."*

- 80% of workers feel stress on the job
- Nearly half of workers say they need more job training
- 14% of respondents say they felt like striking a coworker in the past year, but did not do so
- 25% have felt like screaming or shouting because of job stress
- 10% of American workers are concerned about an individual at work they fear could become violent

FRANK LESLIE RIX

93-year-old Frank Leslie Rix from Great Britain is a lifelong inventor and model maker. He told me he was the first model maker for the (Alexander Graham) Bell phone.

WHEN I WAS in the army in India, many years ago when India was still under British rule, I met a lot of Americans who were stationed in India and they were all always nice and polite. I mean, really, sincerely polite. But the problem was that the Americans had a lot of money in their pockets compared to us Brits. They were very well paid in the American army. They were rich and we were poor, and they liked to show that they had that kind of money, especially to the girls. So, they had a huge advantage over us when it came to impressing the girls with nice and expensive presents. I remember that the Americans threw packets of cigarettes on the floor so we could fight each other to get to them. They did that to impress the girls, and had a lot of fun with it. America was so rich at that time, they could feed the world if they wanted. Later, when I had been in America, (I had been there many times because of my work), I had the same impression. You don't find nicer and more polite people than the Yanks.

When it comes to what I have been doing all my life, innovation, I used to think that we had already invented everything there was to invent. But when I saw a catalog with the entire list of every American invention, I understood that I was totally wrong—Americans invented everything there was to invent. Compared to Americans, we British haven't done anything, and that is really special since America is such a new country if you look at it through European eyes. We Brits had good ideas, but we could never bring them to life due to a lack of money and investors. In America they had everything: money and people with knowledge to produce things. But of course, America benefits from all the nationalities, because it seems that everyone who is good at something has been recruited to work and live in the States.

People should visit America, but beware that Americans are very patriotic. There's nothing wrong with patriotism. Patriotism is very good—nationalism is very bad, beware of it. I actually envy, I mean, sentimentally envy, how each and every American embraces their stars and stripes. Everywhere you go in the States you see their flag flying in gardens, in American houses and at official buildings. They are so proud of it, and they should be. When I first saw a one dollar bill, I looked at it and saw that it says: "In God We Trust." I remember saying, the fact that they print their faith on a dollar note—God will honor that.

The American dream is a wonderful dream, because in England we envy rich people, but in America they don't envy them, instead, they salute them. They recognize that there's something to acknowledge and be proud of when they make it. Americans love success stories. In England we put someone on a pedestal in the hope to be able to knock him off of it. In America if you become wealthy they put you on a pedestal and pat you on the back. I don't remember one instance in my lifetime where we have put somebody on a pedestal and not been glad when somebody else knocks him off of it. We have this jealousy and envy—look at David Beckham! There are parts of the British population that wish he will slip off somehow. Only when he retires will Brits give him some credit for what he has done.

In England it's hard for ordinary people to mix with the rich and noble. The upper crust may acknowledge you if you have something to offer, if there is something you can do for them, but you will never be part of the family.

Please don't misunderstand me, I am pro-royalty and I appreciate royalty. I don't appreciate Prince Charles—I don't like him. He was committing adultery on his marriage night, so I don't like him or his lack of principles. Queen Elizabeth is a wonderful woman. She's a lovely girl from my generation. But Charles and Andrew, they are rotten lath. They are not a good family. We can only hope that William will make a difference.

When I was learning model making, my American boss was Masis Kay Brown, the third. (It's always "the third", like our kings, they always have a number.) My boss was just like a funny little boy when he was riding on the back of my motorbike. I use to take him home and we were the best of friends, and could talk about everything. As soon as he went to work, he was the chief executive officer and you wouldn't dare to take advantage of his friendliness. After work, he was the same "good 'ol boy" again. There was no class consciousness whatsoever, even though he was M.K. Brown "the third." In the UK, in certain areas, the posh people don't mingle with others like they do in America. I remember one time our company had a going away party in a park for one of the executives. On the invitation to the staff it said, please, please wear ordinary clothes because we're playing beer pong. Masis Kay Brown the third and the vice president were both with us and they were so enthusiastic to playing beer pong. Both the Americans, Masis and the vice president, were like two bowery kids. I mean it—it was outstanding, they were playing beer pong like two hooligans in this big posh park – with no class at all. That's how America is! They know how to assert authority, but that is only at work.

Americans are so simple that they are naïve, as well. For them, no place else matters outside the States. They don't think they need the rest of the world. They are such a large country with such a large population that they are self-supplied with everything. They don't even know that we exist, really. We are just part of the rest of the world, of the people who immigrated to their country long ago.

But America is also a funny country, really, where moralists and liberty-fighters go hand in hand. But they are also very ordinary folks, and I hope that they never change.

"You are the greatest sports nation in the world, and it's probably because you all are so stubborn."

Jonathan, Scotland

"Americans like to show that they have money. Especially people who don't have much money, they like to demonstrate that they have a lot of it."

Leonardo, Brazil

MANY SEEM TO HAVE A LOVE AND HATE RELATIONSHIP WITH AMERICA....

I LIKE A LOT about the United States and why shouldn't I? The people are polite, service-minded and friendly, and we all have a chance to make it over there. The American nature is just magnificent.

When I first visited the U.S. I was a bit surprised because the culture was so different. By culture, I mean the sports culture. I didn't meet a single person who didn't talk about anything but sports. And the topic was almost always basketball, American football or baseball. For a foreigner, it was kind of difficult to join in, especially if you didn't know the rules of the game and the name of the players. It was almost impossible to escape from sports talk because I think that every bar and restaurant in America has at least five or six televisions with sports news on them. I still don't understand why they can't show something else or just play some music. But things like that don't irritate me anymore; it's a part of the American culture and when I visit the country now, I quite like it. It gives you an atmosphere of being in America.

The love for traditions and holidays in America is also very admirable, and it seems like everyone is preparing and participating for whatever celebration is next. On the Fourth of July I can see how proud Americans are of their country.

There is not a doubt in my mind that the people in America are different and more outgoing than others in the world, and I mean that everyone can and should learn something from them. While many people in many other countries are shy and afraid to stand out from a crowd, Americans step out and scream, "Hey! Here I am! Choose me!" That is admirable! But there must be a balance and sometimes American drama can be too over-the-top. I don't think I have ever seen an American reality-TV show without a huge theater scene. It's always someone who is ill, or who recently lost a family member or something else sad, and they always seem to mention that the reason they are on that particular TV show is because of them—that they want to honor their loved one or hardship. Then everyone cries and feels so sad. For people outside of America that is a rather strange behavior—all these dramatic scenes on everyday television.

When it comes to good service, Americans are world champions. Many that I have talked to in my travels bring that up in their description of what they like about America. Additionally, in my personal experiences, it is highly unlikely not to get top-level service in America. The customer always comes first, no matter who you are and how you behave. And the workers I meet in America seem really proud of what they do! They appear to genuinely enjoy what they do for a living. That is unusual where I come from, where people often keep their job just to have an income every month, even if they do not enjoy the work.

In general, I would recommend people visit America. Stay there for a while, feel the energy in the country and talk to the people. But I must also recommend that Americans explore their own country much more. Many have rarely ever traveled around, and that is so sad because each and every state is so different that it's like visiting another country, but with the benefits of having the same language. No country in the world has all of these advantages and varied experiences right outside one's front door. Go out and experience your own country - America is full of beauty and adventure, so it would be foolish to have such possibilities outside your doorstep and not benefit from them.

René Zografos

"American guys are way more 'men' than the guys we have back home."

Maria, Mexico

"I have always wondered why so many folks say that they don't like America but still keep traveling back there year after year."

Derek, England

FIVE PEOPLE IN OSLO, NORWAY

"I'm so out-of-focus when I'm driving around in America. All the huge billboards next to the road steal my attention."

Sebastian, Norway

"The only time I eat ketchup is when I'm having pasta. The only time Americans don't eat ketchup seems to be when they're having pasta."

Ellen, Norway

"Except for us Norwegians, Americans are the only ones I know that actually like camping."

Matias, Norway

"Americans have all these friendly, smiley faces. It's really infectious."

Robert, Norway

"We watch so many terrible TV shows back home, and almost every one of them comes from the USA."

Jonas, Norway

AMERICA, THE NEW EMPIRE

MERICA IS LIKE the new empire in the world. Many nations have enormous problems because their highest-educated, young adult residents move to America, yet their expertise is needed back in their home country. But they left because they get paid better in America. That is, of course, beneficial for the Americans who gain these intelligent workers, but fatal for many countries where it is essential to have their own doctors and specialists.

I'm sorry, but I have to be honest and say that I only like one out of every ten Americans I meet. In my opinion, Americans don't seem sincere. Just look at them when they celebrate the holidays; most of them even don't know why they are celebrating. They seem a bit shallow to me; that they are in lack of real culture. They also seem to be lacking when it comes to true knowledge and they appear very selfish. They only care about themselves.

I enjoy sitting down with my family to eat and drink for many hours. For an American, that lengthy mealtime is very strange. They would rather eat alone with a TV or a computer game in front of them. They even eat while they are walking on the street. That can't be healthy for them.

In my opinion, Americans must change their way of thinking; they must learn to value the little things in life.

Americans' philosophy is to live so they can work. We work so we can live, meaning there are other things in life that are more important than working from early morning to late at night every day. What I really like about Americans, though, is that they are problem solvers. It might take time or cost a lot, but they always solve any kind of problem there is to solve.

Vangelis is a travel agent on the Island of Skopelos, Greece

"People in Europe have admired the American system for many years. Now, it seems like the Americans admire the European system."

Linda, France

"Why must the American average Joes act as if they are rock stars? They look very silly."

Sunee, Malaysia

EIGHT AMERICANS ABOUT AMERICA

1) *"America is all about God and money. Money first."*

Aaron

2) *"We are so underfed when it comes to culture. Look to Europe and learn. Actually, look anywhere in the world and learn."*

Judith

3) *"I left my country because it was too full of Americans."*

Katherine

4) "It's very hard for an American to keep his mouth shut; it's quite embarrassing for the few of us who can."

Hugo

5) "In Europe, in general, people think we are awesome. I don't think Americans understand how cool [Europeans] think we are."

Matt

6) "Here is something to think about for us: Americans are concerned about how the world views America, but the world is actually not concerned about how America views them."

Philippe

7) There are many reasons why it's important for foreigners to like us, but I can't think of one good reason why they should—it's quite depressing actually."

Isobel

8) "A common lie in America is that 'all men are equal'."

Vanessa

A FASHION REPORT FROM THE UK

Fashion journalist and trend analyst Dan Hasby-Oliver is one of the most influential fashion authorities in the world. He has worked for top fashion publications as *Adones*, Velour, and *Mode* magazine. He runs "Last Style of Defence," one of the top-visited fashion blogs in the world and also broadcasts his fashion tips on BBC Radio. Here is his fashion report on Americans.

THE AVERAGE AMERICAN guy from most states between California, Texas and New York—states that make up what I call the "U.S. Fashion Triangle"—can be found wearing a similar uniform: Classic-cut denim jeans, a t-shirt or polo shirt and a sweater, zipped or crew-necked. I think the aesthetics of brands like J. Crew, Banana Republic, Tommy Hilfiger, Ralph Lauren and Gap resonate with a guy who wants to assume a sense of style.

I find American fashion and brands have become highly design-led, but with that traditional sense of commerciality that is distilled into design students. I have experienced first-hand students at the Parsons Institute in New York explaining their target retailers and the associated wholesale and retail price points, etc. However, I have seen a change over the past five years toward a look that is becoming more European, sometimes 'London', in the sense of creativity and avant-garde style. Still, the designs retain that pared-back attitude that attracts a self-conscious American consumer.

The distinct difference for me, between American and English menswear, is cut. Following the popularity of Richard Gere, who wore Giorgio Armani suits in American Gigolo, and the likes of

Calvin Klein, who followed him, the relaxed, almost oversized look in the States has been very popular. I think this has something to do with their perceptions of comfort over style but with a desire to retain a sense of formality. English menswear is a lot more tailored, a nod towards the founding Dandies of Jermyn Street and Savile Row - the famed shirting and tailoring streets, respectively, in Central London.

I find the U.K. is an incredible country to focus on the zeitgeist of cool and youth-driven looks, Italy for sartorial, smart looks and the USA for relaxed, laid-back and preppy looks.

The foundations of the preppy style, which was first adopted at Ivy League universities that were swamped by WASP (White Anglo-Saxon Protestant) young men who aspired to the British sensibilities of style. This look is something that was born in the U.S. and has remained in fashion there.

I think the difference between city and countryside style in America depends on the city or state you are in. Firstly, countryside style can be anything from battered jeans and a plaid shirt teamed with a shearling-lined denim jacket to cotton pants and a white crew neck t-shirt. Each look is very comfort-driven but

it depends on the climate, the wearer's fashion sensibilities and the overall understanding of clothing and culture. In terms of cities, the Los Angeles look of slim jeans, low-cut sneakers and a fitted t-shirt is much more stylized than a pair of light-colored khakis topped with a shirt-and-sweater-combo in New York or Boston. I think it is more about attitude and climate than an interpretation of fashion.

I think American girls are very led by trends, but are persuaded by celebrity style. Typically, a pair of bootcut jeans, strapped heels, a fitted t-shirt or a dressy top is an image that I associate with all American girls. There are many social tribes that adhere to an assumed aesthetic and I think that an American woman's look is determined by her personal demographic and lifestyle.

My personal experience of Americans and style is very vast. I spent a week in New York at the Parson's Institute of Design final year student collection review and found their offerings very different, ranging from highly commercial to avant-garde. The city of New York is such a melting pot of people from all over, it is hard to judge its general look, especially because people in America either strive to look better in popular cities or are dressed-down tourists. I find today that business workers are very happy in something smart, but comfortable, unless they buy from European luxury brands that are meant to communicate an image of wealth and power through cut and detail. Los Angeles, though, is a complete polar opposite in that it is very relaxed and while residents there may appear to look unkempt, their fashion choices are highly orchestrated though soft cottons and breathable fabrics. laststyleofdefense.com

"I am not sure that the quality of life has degraded much in the USA. What I am sure of, because of their presence, is that the USA has degraded the quality of life elsewhere."

Peter, England

THREE ON A CRUISE SHIP IN THE MEDITERRANEAN OCEAN

"It's obvious that these cruise ships are built for Americans. They have every form of entertainment, they have exceptional service, the food is free and the ships are so big that you can drive a car inside of them."

Marta, Italy

"Americans have an enormous respect when it comes to celebrities. Back home, we sit and talk to them like any other human being. It's so weird that Americans adore their sports heroes and other celebrities like a holiness every day. Even years after they are retired, many Americans still worship them—forever."

Jan, Netherlands

"It seems to me that the wives have all the command in many American marriages; it can't be any good for the men there."

Leandro, Italy

UP FROM DOWN UNDER

Patrick is an Australian who took a year off from work to travel and to, in his own words, "Discover what's important in life." I met him on a boat in the Indian Ocean.

THE AMERICANS HAVE turned from a "We" to an "I" mentality. Today's American society places enormous demands on all individuals. Much of the pressure comes from social media, where everybody is, and especially the young ones, highly-exposed, whether they are a success or not. To be successful at work, to be fit or beautiful doesn't seem to be enough. There are always higher goals to beat out there, something that will impress others even more. This constant pressure is in all levels of the American society—it's just different types of goals to aim for depending on your social situation. It can be anything from, "Am I invited to the hot fashion show in town?", "Are my friends the right ones to hang out with?", "Do I listen to the right music?", "Do I eat the right food?", "Must I write a blog to fit in?" to "Do I write interesting tweets?". Before social media, it was okay to have a job you personally enjoyed; now, your friends must like it, too, just so you can fit in. I mean, before it was stupid to be fat, today it's completely brainless.

The burden on each and every person is now so much higher if you're not succeeding, because everybody sees you, and judges you. And, of course, everybody wants to show their best side. But that has a price; it makes Americans today very self-focused, and insecure wondering if they're living their life the right way, if they match the standard of today's society, a standard that increases every minute of the day. Americans constantly ask themselves, "What can I do to appear better?" instead of asking themselves, "What can I do to make others feel better so that I can also feel better?"

If Americans turn back from an "I" mentality to a "We" mentality, I'm sure the quality of life will increase radically!

FIVE RANDOM PEOPLE IN STOCKHOLM, SWEDEN

1) *"Everyone is talking air. After hours of conversation, you discover that Americans don't talk about anything."*

Daniel, Sweden

2) *"We don't hate America as a nation; we just hate their attitude toward the rest of the world."*

Karin, Sweden

3) *"Americans are so sensitive and dramatic, but only on TV—it's really too much for us."*

Magnus, Sweden

4) *"Was Twitter what was needed for Americans to discover the rest of the world?"*

Jennie, Sweden

5) *"Americans believe that rest of the world is different from them. Not the other way around."*

Khalid, Sweden

SPOILED AMERICAN KIDS

"The way I see it, spoiled kids are a huge problem in America. I really don't understand why so many parents give away their control to their children and treat them like rulers, as if their own kids should know better than they do about parenting. I believe that all the advice in American media that says and gives so many directions about parenting is very confusing for parents. They should not listen to such random opinions. It is time to take control as a parent and it's time to say no to your kids. Your children will value clear boundaries for what they are allowed to do. This is not only an American problem—in Western Europe I see the same warning signs: spoiled kids who scream or cry their hearts out because the parent tries to talk sense into them instead of taking control of the situation. If American parents will set limits for their kids at an early age, then both the parents and their kids will have a much better life. Having a child can give you enormous energy, and even strength and often a great amount of happiness, but it can also be the other way around if you don't instruct your kids properly.

Iba is a schoolteacher
from Turkey

"It's strange that a society who praises kindness, justice and love through movies and music is so unfriendly, unfair and cold in real life."

Rebecca, England

"It's obvious that America attracts the best people in the world in any genre or category, but I don't know why."

Lisa, Australia

"American men are so much more healthy, nice and fit than our men. They don't need to empty the whole vodka bottle as quick as they can, like all the Russian men do!"

Valoura, Russia

"America is a country where it is essential to be rich or famous, preferably both."

Luke, Costa Rica

THE WORLD VS. THE USA

On May 8, 2013, Gunnar Garfors completed his quest to visit every country in the world. Here is what he thinks about how the USA compares to the rest of the world.

I HAVE CERTAINLY CHANGED my opinion about the U.S. after my world travels.

I was an exchange student in Indiana from 1992 to 1993. Back then, the United States embodied the American dream to me. I had a fantastic time, met many friends and learned a lot about the country, about the language, about different cultures and about myself. I was still very much in awe after the year there, and I returned again in 1997 when I interned for two months at CNN in Washington, D.C. I have now developed more of a love-hate relationship with the country. There are still many things I enjoy: the differences, the nature, my friends and people I knew briefly or merely know of. What really gets to me is their attitude toward the rest of the world, and their way of being— I am now speaking in stereotypes. Too many Americans come across as very superficial and speak largely in clichés and memorized phrases. Of course, you can say it is better that people are friendly, even if they don't mean it, than shy or impolite, but I appreciate people being frank and earnest. Unfortunately, I have not experienced that from the majority of Americans I've met. Furthermore, they are not up to speed on what happens outside their own country, often not even what happens outside their own state. Being there as a foreigner and being asked so many uninformed questions can be frustrating to many. Luckily, I usually manage to see the funny side of it, but it makes me wonder how much longer the country can remain a super power. As the well-known phrase goes, "Know your friends and know your enemies, or cease to matter."

Americans should drop their arrogance and superficiality. Those two features will dethrone them as a superpower unless they are addressed. Not acknowledging the importance of the rest of the world is a big mistake; and believing that you are always number one never leads to anything good.

We don't need to travel far away from the U.S. to feel the differences—it's quite a noticeable difference between the U.S. and Canada. Canada's "European connection" seems to have influenced the country and they appear more internationally-minded than U.S. citizens. I have spent less time in Mexico, but I still feel that there is a difference in atmosphere there. In a phrase, there is less arrogance among the two neighbors of the U.S. than in the country between them.

However, I do enjoy American hospitality and how open many Americans are to other people. Americans are, overall, very polite, except when it comes to foreign politics. What I do not like is that their openness and hospitality seems to be limited to a certain point. And it is hard to feel truly welcome due to their superficiality. Also, the openness seems to be much greater on home turf than when traveling, strangely enough.

There are so many amazing countries and incredible people with unique characteristics out there. I used to rate countries after visiting them, but I have traveled so much that it is hard to rank them now. However, I still group countries according to my own preferences. The U.S. would be above the middle rankings, but certainly not in my top group. And there is, in all honesty, no country that I would not go back to, given the opportunity. That being said, I am not a huge fan of countries where religion has too much of an impact on society, in particular the extremist views of some areas and any religion that calls for discrimination against certain people, most often women. I see this far too often in Muslim countries. Let's use parts of Afghanistan as an example—women dressed in very modern ways, with fashions that probably rivaled the U.S., back in the 70s. Now, they can't even be on the street without a burqa. Awful! As a rule, I do not like double standards. Jokingly, I'd say that the Vatican is one of my least favorite countries because there are only old men there, and no bars.

I think Australia and South Africa are similar to the States because they all have elements of American culture. Family seems to be important in all three, as is individuality. I get some of the same feelings when I am in these two countries as I do in the U.S. Americans would feel at home in Brazil and Argentina thanks to their massive size, in Japan and South Korea for the convenience and high-level of service and in Iceland and Norway for the beautiful scenery. However, Norwegians are actually quite rude—not because they necessarily want to be, more because of shyness. Also, Chinese may come across as rather impolite to Westerners. Then again, there are 1.3 billion of them, so they can't really afford the time to be nice to everyone. I'd say that the Americans and the British are among the most polite people in the world.

Countries like Nauru (the world's smallest republic) have almost no services to offer, so very few U.S. citizens would enjoy it there for more than a few days.

AMERICAN EXPLORERS

NORWEGIANS TRAVEL LIKE crazy—the average Norwegian now spends twice as much on travels as the average Swede, who also travels frequently. The problem is that too many Norwegians are happy going to the same places—as long as there is a beach and a bar, they seem happy. I find that rather sad. Where has the curiosity gone? Norway is a nation of explorers. Of course, the British and French have also explored the world, so they certainly should not be forgotten, but the percentage of people traveling in those countries is smaller. The U.S. is awful in terms of international travel. Some Americans travel a lot, of course, and they are true explorers, but just look at the percentage of Americans who own a passport. It is so low, it's scary.

Traveling Americans do usually have more insight about other countries and international relations skills than those who do not travel at all. They have seen different cultures and at least understand that there is a difference between the U.S. and the rest of the world. However, many of them still seem to strongly favor the American way of life and do not seem open to new impressions. They are not spontaneous—they seem to be rather traditionally minded and like to plan ahead. Impulsiveness is a skill, and an underrated one at that. I may sound negative now, but, again, I must emphasize that I am stereotyping. There are Americans that I know who do not comply with these characteristics; unfortunately, they are vastly outnumbered.

In the U.S., I like the possibilities with regards to what to see and what to do. But there are a lot of differences between different states. Many Americans move often between states though, and this factor may play down those differences a bit. There are still certain

U.S. characteristics that do seem to be in place, regardless of one's hometown. The sheer size of the country and the fact that most of it is inhabited opens up the possibility to see a range of traditions and cultures. That also means that almost everything can be found there: glaciers, deserts, mountains, plains, lakes, oceans, hills, farmland, rivers, streams, islands, waterfalls and so much more.

The U.S. is generally a great country for experiencing excellent service, but Asia is catching up. Even though the service is excellent, the tipping culture in the U.S. is awful. You kind of get the sense that people are friendly and service-minded, but only because they know that you will pay a large tip. That takes away the sincerity of the service.

The U.S. is a great country for tourists as the service levels are high and the prices are comparatively low. It has, however, gone a little too far, so nothing seems real anymore; because everything is cater to paying tourists. I resent American tourist attractions, but I love the different scenery, the nature experiences and seeing typical U.S. villages, towns and neighborhoods.

Here is why people should visit the U.S.: excellent service, high standards of facilities, variety and you know what to expect.

Here is why people should not visit the U.S.: lack of excitement, tipping-based service and virtually no gun laws.

Compared to many other countries, the U.S. is huge, but their dominance within literature and filmmaking, and the previously stated openness to immigration from virtually all nations have cemented a certain U.S. way of being. Maybe the superficiality is a way of keeping a necessary distance from others. I would prefer to see the people of the U.S. take a greater interest in the rest of the world. It is strange to me that people in a country made up of so many nationalities show so little interest for what happens outside their borders.

I am very adaptable and I could live pretty much anywhere. I do, however, prefer to live near the sea, along a coastline, if I were to live somewhere for a long time. I have lived in the U.S. twice, and it is not at the top of my list for places I would wish to live in again. However, I would still be open to move there if a very exciting job opportunity came around.

Seattle is my number one city in the U.S., followed by San Francisco. New York City is a solid number three on my list. I enjoy nature and the sea, and New York is in many ways a nutshell of urban USA, but still with a fair amount of European influence. I must add that I have never been to Boston, although I suspect that Boston will be my very favorite when I finally do visit.

People in the U.S. are very materialistic, but new countries are rapidly catching up, especially fast-growing Asian economies and Russia. But the U.S. has, for a long time, hurt its own economy by their race for profits. To save short-term dollars, they have given up on maintaining their skills and their unique position of being seen as the best. Their pride of driving U.S.-made vehicles and consuming U.S.-made goods seems to have gone away. Now they seem unable to turn that trend around.

The people of the U.S. have not only exported workplaces, but also skills, competence and pride, just to be able to buy cheaper. But what has happened as a result? There is not enough work back home. Capitalism may be a good thing for the U.S., but not when it undermines the ability of the country's own citizens to contribute to the economy, and, at the same time, it deprives the country of its skill set.

Just one more thing that I think is worth mentioning—it is quite misleading that everyone assumes that "American" means someone or something from the USA. There are 23 countries in North America and 12 in South America. Anyone from any of these countries is American, although the U.S. has sort of monopolized the term. Therefore, I try not to use the term "American" when speaking about people or products from the U.S. It's just a small protest from me, but I do still think that this way of using the word says something about the U.S. mentality and the previously mentioned arrogance. garfors.com

"Family first! I like the "built-in" loyalty Americans have for their family."

Michael, Switzerland

"Many American men pretend that they have good self-esteem, but it is not trustworthy for those of us who see it from outside."

Lars, Germany

"I haven't met an American who did not believe that everyone else was happier than himself."

Corinne, France

SURF'S UP

I TRAVELED QUITE A bit during my younger days when I was a professional surfer. Throughout my travels, there was always a stigma that Americans are loud and obnoxious people. I must say that not all Americans I encountered were that way. I was far more taken aback by the Brazilians' loud, brash, cocky approach. We have dealt with rude and obnoxious people from all over the world. But in general we have had extremely friendly and kind people visit us from Europe. When we get Americans visiting us, we don't have too many issues with them, fortunately.

About 70 percent of our guests come from the USA, 15 percent are from Canada, 10 percent are from the UK and the remaining 5 percent are from elsewhere around the world.

We tend to attract pretty relaxed and cool Americans looking to learn how to surf. But, I would still like to give advice to the Americans: treat people the way you would want to be treated, and remember, it is always better to give than it is to receive!

Americans are also a little more detail-oriented than others in terms of planning their trip to visit us. I find that a lot of the guests from the U.S. like to get in shape physically prior to visiting to ensure they get the most out of their time with us.

The most talented surfers typically have the most consistent and good surf experience. I would say that the world's best surfers are coming from America (including Hawaiians), Australia and, with surfing's surge in popularity, Indonesia. Being a surfer is a gift and the fact that we can go out and enjoy nature and harness its power is a blessing only a small fraction of the world population will ever get to experience. I don't see nationality when I meet other surfers, I just see surfers. And most of us have a common goal—freedom.

Tim Marsh, owns the Safari Surf School in Costa Rica

"Americans like to impress their neighbors. It doesn't matter what it takes—they shall and must impress them."

Caroline, Belgium

"'That's what the women are for!' —I'm talking about the mentality of American men when it comes to housework."

Kirsten, Denmark

"Americans talk and talk, and I adore that! You may take it for granted, but in many other places people hardly speak to each other. So to hear Americans doing all that talking is just wonderful."

Victoria, Bulgaria

THREE ON FUERTEVENTURA, A SPANISH ISLAND

1) *"In America they have so much water in their toilets that they should give us towels after a visit in their restroom—it always splashes up too much."*

Francesco, Spain

2) *"A lot of people say that they don't like America. But what surprises me is that they can't explain why. It seems like it is the right thing to say. Even though they don't have any knowledge about America or Americans, they will still continue to say that they don't like them. It's an absolutely ridiculous behavior."*

Kamal, Morocco

3) *"I always dreamed of going to America, but once I got there on my first visit, I started to have a new dream—to go back home. Spain has more sincere people. I can't live in a fake world like America."*

Matilde, Spain

THE REMOTE AMERICAN DREAM

Evan Lewis is an American beer brewer who went to Europe to find the American dream.

I DON'T MISS MUCH about America. But there is a certain sense of freedom in the U.S. In Norway, where I live now, and also the rest of Europe, it is a slightly more restrictive society in some ways.

One thing I do miss about America is normal taxes on cars. Goods and services in the States are less expensive, and there is easy access to these things.

If I had to pick two differences to point out it would be health care and labor. The American health system is excellent, and you have a lot of freedom to choose your doctor. If you need to see a specialist today, no problem, as long as you can pay for it. However, fifty million people don't have any health insurance in the U.S., and for those people all the freedom of choice in the world doesn't help. [Author's note: This statistic may have changed due to the emergence of Obamacare.] To top it off, the average American doesn't want to make the system any better. In most of Europe we have health care for all, but very little freedom to choose within the public system.

With regard to labor, the U.S. and Europe are complete opposites. In the U.S. the employer has all the power and the employee has very little. 'Do your job well or lose it' is the basic understanding. Employees have no right to vacation time if the employer doesn't offer it, except for some public holidays, about ten days per year. In Norway and some other countries in Europe, the employee has all the rights and benefits while the employer is looked upon as the 'big bad wolf'.

Americans are generally hard workers, who take pride in doing a good job and finishing the job. Europeans are more concerned with leaving work on time and getting enough vacation and less concerned about giving good service or the job itself.

It takes time to learn the business culture and customs in a foreign country, especially if you have a business with employees. Labor laws are very important to understand, and basic challenges like language and who to call for goods and services are initial roadblocks for doing business in other countries. Businesses in America get many benefits in terms of tax relief and liberal labor laws that simply don't exist in many European countries.

"Looking around it seems that American food has fairly well invaded Europe—at least if you count in burgers and fries."

Evan Lewis, an emigrated American

In many ways, I believe in the American dream; though, I am somewhat cynical. The American dream is based on the idea that hard work and determination will allow an individual to achieve prosperity, regardless of that person's background or education. The measurement of prosperity or achievement naturally varies from person to person, but is most often associated with acquisition of material goods like a car or a house.

The meaning of the American dream has changed over the decades. While Americans are generally ambitious, hard workers, many people work just to have more material things, better things or the same things as their neighbors. It is woven into the very fabric of the American people to work hard, get a better job, get promoted, start a business, buy a house, buy a bigger house and so on, and so on and so on.

I'm a business owner and a capitalist in many ways. I work very hard and am proud of my achievements. I have experienced failure in spite of hard work, and I have experienced success. In the midst of a failure, I would tell you "nothing ventured, nothing gained," that you don't achieve if you don't try. Sometimes you succeed and sometimes you don't, but as an ambitious American, it is in my blood to work hard and achieve. In these ways, I believe in the American dream. At the same time I realize that eternal pursuit of greater achievements leads many people to feel dissatisfied. For some Americans, the dream is simply not reachable based on where they live, the job they hold or that they are simply never satisfied.

EVAN ABOUT AMERICAN BEER

THE AMERICAN BEER scene consists of a few very large breweries making undrinkable cheap lager. That's 90 percent of the beer consumed in the U.S., and unfortunately, all that most foreigners seem to know about it. The reality is that the other 10 percent is "craft beer," in other words, beer from the microbreweries. There are nearly nineteen hundred small breweries in the U.S., making an enormous diversity of fantastic handcrafted brews. That 10 percent is a huge market and is responsible for the craft brewing revolution worldwide.

EVAN ABOUT DRINKING

IN MY EXPERIENCE there is a strong culture among the American adult population for enjoying a drink or two with friends after work, or with a meal out or at home. For most people, this is just social and part of enjoying life, and the majority of these adults aren't binge drinkers. In the USA, it is acceptable to have a drink on any night of the week in this way, without participating in binge drinking on the weekends. For many Europeans, on the other hand, binge drinking is more normal regardless of age, while a social drink on a weekday is less common.

"If you take an American out of his home environment, he can actually be nice."

Lisa, Slovakia

"The Americans judge me so fast and tell me what type of person I am, long before we have been introduced to each other properly."

Gareth, Wales

FIVE PEOPLE IN NICE, FRANCE

"It's always the future that's important for an American. Their own goals, far away from now, are all that matters. They should enjoy the days that are here more."

Olivia, France

"Americans are very careful with spending their own money, but love to spend others'. Americans are a bit cheap to me."

Patricia, France

"Why can't Americans swear on TV? They do it anyway in everyday life."

Charlotte, France

"A gentleman is rarely an American."

Coline, France

"I remember some of the hotels in America had advertisements that say: "We have clean hotel rooms." So I have always wondered, isn't it normal to have clean rooms in America?"

Khumar, France

FROM A STYLIST'S VIEW

Laia Faran is a British stylist who has worked for magazines like Vogue and Marie Claire, and celebrities such as Britney Spears, Jordan, Ben Eton and Carmen Electra

COMPARED TO AMERICANS, Italian men are very elegant. Italian fashion is very much a part of the Italian culture; their attention to detail and good quality materials are so fundamental to Italians that anything below that would be unacceptable to them. But, I think Italian men are very proud and self-conscious, and look more after their grooming and image in general compared to Americans.

In my opinion, Americans will go further than Europeans to achieve perfection (i.e. plastic surgery). Regarding plastic surgery, I think Americans are undergoing invasive treatments more often and at younger ages nowadays, and that is not advisable. A lot can be achieved with non-invasive treatments and diets.

When it comes to hairstyles, I'm sure some areas such as Texas appear to have an aesthetic that is, perhaps, similar to '80s fashion, but other places such as Hollywood couldn't be further from that.

As the world has become a global village, fashion has integrated in such a way that what once were clear differences have now been eradicated.

Ultimately, I think happiness takes years off people!

"Hip hoppers in saggy pants with huge gold necklaces around their neck—that's what first comes to my mind when I think of Americans."

Sarah, Germany

"Most of the American guys just dress in whatever they can find. My guess is that they don't care what they wear as long as they feel comfortable and can have on their baseball cap. But on the other side, you also have these American men who dress for success, who really dress up to perfection with extraordinary style. Sadly, there are not many of them left there."

Dayras, Belgium

OBSERVATIONS FROM A VAGABOND

WHEN I MEET Americans in America, they all seem to be on autopilot. It's like I'm talking to machines. If you walk into a store, you will hear something like: "Welcome, sir. How are you, sir?" Five seconds later, the next customer that comes in hears the exact same phrase. The facial expressions are the same, no matter who comes in the door. It's not like they aren't smiling, it's more like they are smiling without being sincere. They turn so polite that it's not believable. It can really be frustrating for us, thinking: "Are they really nice or not?" But after a day out on the town, shopping and eating out, you will find out that they are all on the same autopilot. It doesn't feel sincere at all for us Europeans. We are used to nice and not nice people, people who smile and don't smile, people who are in different moods at home and at work. In America, everyone seems to be the same person, no matter what mood they are in that particular day. It's like I can't reach them. The true American, in my opinion, you won't find in America; they are everywhere else in the world. Because when you meet Americans abroad, you find them totally different—the autopilot is gone. Some talk a lot, while some are, believe it or not, actually just silent. Some drink too much and act a bit foolish like the rest of us, but they all share what they feel and show what mood they are in. It's like they are joining the rest of us in the big family of people called the world. I love to meet Americans outside of their own country where they are like humans who act like humans, no matter what mood they are in.

Günther, Germany, travels the world

"American families often believe that their neighbors have a better life than they do. They measure their own happiness on how their neighbors' status compares to their own."

Mariie, Italy

"Gamblers, Christians wearing guns on the street, billionaires among the beggars—it only exists in this weird world called America."

Janeke, Netherlands

"Why are Americans so suspicious of everything that is new to them?"

Ranjeet, India, lives in England

HOW TO ACHIEVE SUCCESS IN AMERICA

Pelle Lidell knows the music and show business industry throughout the world. At the age of 18, he started as a full-time musician. Later, he worked as an A&R [someone responsible for talent scouting and overseeing the artistic development of recording artists and/or songwriters] and a scout for EMI in Los Angeles. He is also a sports freak and has been playing all kinds of sports his whole life. He is the judge of Swedish Idol and is the European A&R executive for Universal Music.

AMERICAN SPORTS

I love American sports, and most of all I like baseball. I am one of the few who has actually played baseball in Sweden. But it's not surprising to me that the sport isn't bigger across the world; the sport itself is too slow and boring to watch. Baseball, American football and those kinds of sports will not work here in Europe. Look at American football, for example—it has way too many breaks during a game for it to be interesting to watch.

American baseball is part of America's heritage. American's have baseball in the blood, from little league up to adulthood. And to be honest, soccer in America is not going to be a dominant sport either. American athletes can, of course, have some years they are good, but to be a great sports nation,

DID YOU KNOW?

The average NFL game has just ten minutes and forty-three seconds of broadcasted game play. Most of the time, (sixty-seven minutes) is spent with the players standing around, while, on average, only three seconds are spent showing the cheerleaders.

the sport must be included in the cultural heritage, and soccer is not a part of that in America. With that said, if we look at it from another perspective, America is really a good sports nation, especially in ball sports. So, if they would really go for it, they could be good in some ball sports that are big in Europe and Asia, like handball. I am sure that America could have the world domination in handball if they would aim for it, because look at the potential they have at their colleges, and the ball handling they demonstrate in other sports, like basketball. But again, it has to be a part of their sport culture to achieve international success. Money also matters. Why is basketball such a big sport in America? Because it doesn't cost anything to play it. There are basketball hoops everywhere. You can play with up to ten players ("five on five") or as few as four ("two on two"). You can meet that competitive level no matter where you live in America. With baseball, it's the same thing: all you need is a glove, a bat and a ball, and you're out the door practicing.

AMERICAN MUSIC

T O UNDERSTAND THE difference between American pop music and the rest of the world, we have to look at the radio stations. In America, the radio stations play music by the genre. One station plays only rock, another station plays adult contemporary, and so forth. European radio, on the other hand, plays pop music and many other genres on the same station. In Europe, you can hear hip-hop, a dance song and a country song on the same channel. We have radio stations where all the popular styles are blended together.

European pop music is more eclectic than American pop, and English pop music is much more innovative as compared to American pop music. It's more "cutting edge" here; we easily mix the different music styles together so we can bring something new to the table. A band like The Prodigy could never come from the U.S. But it's not the American musicians' fault; there's a lot of creativity there, but they have to adjust to what the radio stations want to play. There are also huge differences inside the U.S. For example, Moby couldn't come from Kansas or somewhere else, he could only be from New York. On the other hand, there are exceptions, and they almost always come from working class cities. It's very interesting to look at Pharrell Williams and the N.E.R.D. boys because they are from Virginia. They were pretty cutting edge during the height of their popularity. Another example is the Atlanta, Georgia music scene with Outkast and others. Look at Detroit, too, a working class city. It's not surprising that punk rock and house music started out in Detroit. It's also the same in other countries, in cities like Manchester and Glasgow. These are working class cities that have provided us with legendary music. In contrast, New York and L.A. are not working class cities. Why did "grunge" music come from Seattle? Because it is a working class city. America's music is also ethnically influenced. In the beginning of the rise of hip-hop, there weren't many white Americans who listened to it. That has all changed.

> **"It's very hard to br`eak into the music business in America, but the normal way to do it is to first go local, then regional, and finally national."**
>
> **Pelle Lidell**

The challenge today for an American musician is to be creative and new, and at the same time make sure that their sound is palatable for the commercial American radio stations. However, if you are in it for the money, you don't normally take such creative risks; it's a lot safer to do something like Justin Bieber has done and go all in on a very commercially appealing sound.

If I were a young American musician today looking for success, I would focus on networking—it's the most important thing. Build your own network of fans. Second, you need to incorporate your hometown roots into the music, be yourself and then you will have an edge, and be able to create something that not every Yankee has. I would also pick songs that work for the American market, but at the same time sound a bit different. All the hits I have had in the U.S. are songs that work in the American market, but, at the same time, sound a bit different. You must create something that comes from inside you. For example, we, from the Nordic countries, have a melancholic sense of melody. Since we are that way, we use it in our music. Look at the international artists who have made it in America: from Sinead O'Connor in the earlier days to today's Adele, Coldplay or U2. All of them have one thing in common—they've never made a happy pop song, even though American and European music have grown similar in sound over the last ten years. The types of songs these artists produce always have a beautiful, epic feeling.

In other words, if you shall sell something to the Yankees, you must bring something to the table they don't already have.

American artists are, musically, among the best in the world. The reason for this is that the entertainment industry in the USA has grown so big over many years. Americans have a long tradition of utilizing music managers and agents, and the overall industry is older in America than in other parts of the world. This attracts top international talent to join the American entertainment industry because it's more lucrative than elsewhere. Twenty-five years ago, if you said you work in the music business, not many people would look positively on you, but that has changed. Today, the music business is super professional.

When it comes to illegal downloading, Americans still steal about 30 to 35 percent of their music. For me, that is very surprising. It seems like many Americans steal from the artist only because they can. In the beginning of the music downloading era, illegally downloading music was more easily understood, because the music they wanted wasn't easily obtainable by purchase. Now, that is no longer the case. I would never download a movie without paying for it just because I can, as that would make me a thief. But to be honest, illegal downloading started with stubborn, protective record companies who wouldn't deal with the new technology, like Napster and similar movements. They really made the customers angry, and they acted like ostriches with their heads buried in the dirt as they said, "This is not happening." They didn't want to deal with the reality that the new technology was here to stay. And to be honest, many of the American music executives made money like oil barons, as compared to the profits you would have found in other companies' results. So people started to say, "Fuck you—I can download it free, so why should I pay for their luxuries?" In addition, music companies rushed to release records with maybe only two good songs on it, just to get good results in the specific period of time the album was released. They had a budget to follow and they didn't care that the customers only got two good songs on a full-length album, as long as it brought good money in for the company. Now you can get those two good songs from iTunes, and skip the rest of the album, but that has also killed the album. So, the record company executives in the U.S. really shot themselves in the foot.

ABOUT THE USA

I DON'T FEEL LIKE an outsider when I am in the USA. I understand the USA; I know how to behave there. I look at and talk with Americans the same way I do with people in Europe. Even compared to Asia, the U.S. isn't much different anymore.

But I also have to say something about the American city that I lived in. All honor to Los Angeles, but it's not that cool of a town or a great place to live; it's like a gigantic suburb. Everyday life is absolutely not better there. Plus, I love the four seasons throughout the year that I have where I live now, from charming rainy days to sunny mornings. Sometimes, when I wake up in the morning, I think, "Wow, what a beautiful sunny day." I never felt that in L.A.; there it was more like, "Shit, another boiling day in the suburb."

I also don't like that Americans are the most overweight people in the world, and that is not because they have a higher standard of living. The way they showcase junk food on TV is just depressing, and I find it really disgusting. I get so upset about that! And look what costs they pass on to the society—where I come from, we make rules for our kids, candy and soda is only allowed on Saturdays.

THE AMERICAN DREAM

AMERICANS HAVE HIGHER ambitions than anyone else. They are goal setters and "go getters". They have been fed with the American dream in their mother's milk. The reality of the American dream is still attainable, but it's harder to achieve now than ever before. It's a whole different reality in America today than it used to be. And Americans don't have solidarity thinking, like we have in Europe. An example of this is national health care for everyone, whereas Americans think that is a communistic or a socialistic idea. That is not the case at all; national health care is a humanistic idea. Would you like to live in a society, with a tunnel view, that says, "Fuck all the rest, as long as I am fine"? So America, there you have something to learn. You can be ultra rich in the USA because the market is so big, but if you look at the country where I come from, where everybody has the same possibilities in life, we have a much better world to live in. Our citizens have a very good quality of life, we can choose the schools we want, if we get sick, we get help and we get paid. If you fuck up in life, you can get back on track and have a new education and start over without any extra expense. I'm a working class guy myself, and every opportunity is here for me and everyone else. I really wish that Americans could have the same opportunities as we have in life.

"The use of the word 'dude' makes Americans look very stupid."

Christian, Switzerland

"Is it true that America has TV shows for dogs? What's next, McDonald's drive-in for cats?"

Jaan, Estonia

FOUR IN EGYPT

"My advice to the Americans that travel is to be "less American" because the mentality of being better than others can cause them problems."

Baba, Kairo

"I want freedom, and my dream is to live as an American. I don't know if Americans know how lucky they are, that they are born in a country with all the possibilities in life and that they have freedom, real freedom."

Hala, Luxor

"It's so weird, but the American garbage disposals really make the garbage disappear!"

Sanae, Alexandria

"It's really smart that Americans practice the sports that nobody else in the world does—that way they can always win."

Monhammed, Luxor

"Looks like every kid in America strives to audition for American Idol. To us, they appear desperate."

Jose, Paraguay

"Americans are remarkably creative. I don't know of any other place in the world where you can find as many creative people as you do in the U.S. It's very admirable."

Melik, Turkey

MY FIRST DAY IN "BIG" AMERICA

O N MY FIRST trip to America in 1994, I didn't know what to expect. All I knew about America was what I had seen on television or read in magazines. My friend and I had planned our trip to America for quite a while, and the places we had decided to visit were as follows: Houston, Austin, San Antonio, Las Vegas, San Francisco, Los Angeles and San Diego. Overall, I can say that the whole trip was an adventure, but this little story comes from the first few hours of our very first day in "Big America."

When we arrived at the airport in the outskirts of Houston, you could say that everything was different from what we were used to. The distance between everything was enormous. Shortly after our first steps on the American continent, we felt so tiny in that gigantic country. There were so many people to see, and so many new things to look at! At first, we couldn't even find our rental car, but after about an hour of searching, we finally understood that the rental car was not parked at the airport like we were used to back home. The rental company actually picked us up in a bus and drove us to the car. We arrived at the parking lot, or should I say, the parking field—it must have been thousands of cars, like several soccer fields filled with cars. At that point we already had some idea of the size of the country we were in, but there was more to come!

My friend gave me the honor of driving the car into the center of Houston to find a hotel. Our final goal for the day was an area of town called The Galleria. We decided to go there after talking to the girl sitting next to me on the airplane. She told us that The Galleria area was a perfect starting point for our holiday. The driving went pretty well, but my friend, the map-reader, had problems. First of all, there were so many roads to choose from, and sometimes we came to crossroads with several roads in layers above us, each going in a different direction. It was literally like being in a science fiction movie. On top of the map confusion and crazy crossroads, it wasn't the easiest task to finally pull out of the main road into downtown Houston. Of course, there had to be around seven, eight or maybe even more roads to choose from to get in to downtown Houston. Finally, after several hours of driving around, we found a hotel, a Holiday Inn in the recommended Galleria area.

After relaxing a bit at the hotel, we were ready for a night on the town. First, we visited a Mexican restaurant that had really good, tasty food. A bit later, with stomachs full of Mexican food and beer, we paid a visit to a blues club. At the entrance to the club, we couldn't believe our eyes; there sat the largest, or should I say the widest, man I have ever seen in my life. He actually sat on a sofa instead of a chair, collecting money from visitors at the entrance. He literally filled the whole sofa. I wouldn't believe it if I hadn't seen it in person. I have never seen a man that fat in my entire life, and still haven't seen a man as big since then, not even on TV!

There weren't a lot of people inside the club, but we met two American girls immediately, and they had absolutely no shyness or fear in talking to us. They actually both insisted on buying us the first round of drinks, some shots. That alone is something that rarely happens where I come from. In my country, the boys must dig deep in their pockets to please a girl. After a while, one of the girls, named Laura, said that there was a great club close by that we should go visit, so the four of us decided to go and check it out. Only minutes later, when we arrived to the place that Laura had recommended, my friend and I had to smile, because we had just been there for a beer earlier, after our feast of Mexican food. During our first visit, there weren't more than two or three customers inside. But that had all changed now that it was later in the evening. There was an enormous queue of customers waiting to get in. I figured that if we waited, it would take all night to get inside, that is, if we got in at all. As naïve Norwegians, we decided to pass up the queue and try to walk right in ahead of all the other guests. Laura was a bit afraid of doing that and tried to stop us, but she was too late because we were already there, right at the front door. The tall doorman said, "Welcome, sir," to both me, and my friend, but stopped the girls from coming in. After we quickly explained to the doorman that the girls were with us, he also let them in. I guess they recognized us from earlier. To everyone's surprise, we discovered all these big and very tall guys in the club. My friend and I talked a bit about it, and we actually questioned ourselves, "Is this what the average American guys look like? Are they really that much taller than any other human being we have ever seen?" The American boys looked like gigantic creatures from outer space. We had never seen taller men anywhere in the world, but there was a logical explanation.

After a short while, we found out that the Houston Rockets basketball team had just won the NBA final, and that the whole team and their friends were there to celebrate the championship. No wonder there was a big line outside.

After way too many drinks, my friend wanted to go home, but I wasn't ready to leave. He said he could take a taxi and he told me to stay and have fun. About an hour or so later, I also decided to leave the place and only minutes later, I arrived at our hotel, which was located quite nearby. But I discovered that my friend hadn't come back yet, I found that very strange since it was only a few minutes away by car and more than an hour had passed since he left the club. I was so certain he would be back at his room long before I got there.

My friend has a Norwegian name, Asbjorn. In Norwegian, the ending of that name means bear, so Bjorn means bear.

When Asbjorn took the taxi, he told the driver to go to "Holiday Inn". The driver asked, "Which one?" Asbjorn didn't understand the taxi driver's question because he thought that there was only one Holiday Inn hotel in all of Houston, and so he just kept saying, "Go to Holiday Inn."

The poor taxi driver had no choice but to start driving to quite a lot of Holiday Inn hotels in Houston so that Asbjorn could figure out where he was staying. But there was another problem—Asbjorn didn't remember what the hotel building looked like from the outside, or from the inside, for that matter, so every time he came to a new hotel, he had to go in to the front desk at the hotel and ask the receptionist, "Do I stay here?" And to be helpful, he translated his name into English so they could understand him better, or so he thought. So, the question to the receptionists from Asbjorn was, "My name is Ass-Bear, do I live here?"

It took him seven different Holiday Inn hotels before he finally found out where he was staying and could jump into bed.

Every experience in America has, for me, been really, really big in every meaning of the word. And that first day was no exception. The big parking field, the wide, big guy, the big line to come in the club, the tall people, the big city with all the hotels with the same names, all the winding roads, the people with big dreams and a lot, lot more.

You can only imagine all the great moments I have had there since my first arrival. The all-magnificent, but also kind of strange people I met there, the never-ending, breathtaking scenery the country has to offer and the huge tempo of society that you only find there. It's for sure a big circus over there, in America, but who doesn't like to go to the circus? I don't mind, and I'm definitely looking forward to my next one.

René Zografos

"High superlatives, like 'super great', 'awesome' and 'so amazing' seems to be on every American's tongue."

Francisco, Argentina

"I can summarize my meetings with the American people in one word: cold."

Mahmut, Turkey

"Americans are very funny, but unfortunately, often their humor is on others' behalf. They often make hurtful comments about someone else to make others laugh."

Jan, Netherlands

"American women are very liberated, but very good at hiding it from their families. When we see these girls in Italy, the Italian men don't need to use much effort to pick them up."

Isabella, Italy

EIGHT FROM ENGLAND ABOUT AMERICA

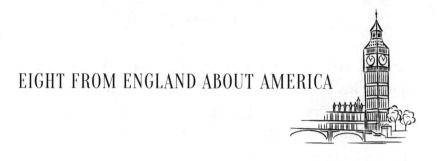

1) *"I like the American accent—so confident, so strange, so sexy."*

> Hannah, England

2) *"Way too many people doing drugs there. It's like, "Have a cocaine and a smile."*

> Jason, England

3) *"America is exactly like a big brother to me, in every aspect of what a big brother means: a lot good, but more bad."*

> Gabby, England

4) *"Americans talk so incredibly loud, like they are the only persons in the room."*

> Amy, England

5) *"Even if everything is really bad in their life, Americans will still pretend that everything is just fine—they are just very good at hiding it."*

> Trevor, England

6) *"I spent years living in America, and when I go out there, I rarely come across a man I fancy. I think that the majority of the guys there are either fat, ugly, annoying or a mixture of all three."*

Lisa, England

7) *"When I first went there, I understood that I had too romantic of a view about America."*

Myra, England

8) *"America is one of the few countries where you can make money and have success, and it's all good for everyone else. They even salute you for it."*

Damon, England

GREETINGS FROM CANADA

"My best advice to Americans who travel abroad is to pretend that they are Canadians; people will then wish them a warm welcome. I'm being deathly honest when I say, people all over the world like Canadians a lot more. It's the naked truth."

Charles, Canada

"Americans talk the talk, and actually walk the walk. And that is exactly what we should do, too, but we are normally too cowardly to finish what we started."

Louise, Canada

"Many Americans, in general, are very capitalistic, but many, in fact, still live like they do in a banana republic."

Brett, Canada

"I'm sure that Canadians, deep inside, believe that America is a fantastic country. Even though it is very, very hard for them to admit sometimes."

Monty, Canada

"I've always loved beautiful and artistic things, but before leaving America I had very little chance of seeing any."

Emma Albani, legendary soprano from Canada

FAT AND FATTER

"American cookies actually taste like plain sugar. They're not edible for my taste. All these cookies full of sugar make me nauseous, and they must make Americans chubby."

Jaqueline, Brazil

"Even when they are full, many Americans have to eat more. They just bring the doggy bag home, where nobody can see them."

Tamara, Netherland

"Sugar in the morning, sugar in the evening means fat Americans in the end."

Joel, England

 DID YOU KNOW?

Americans are fat, and getting fatter. If Americans continue their current lifestyles, 83 percent of men will be overweight by 2020. Women are right behind them, with 72 percent predicted to be overweight, or obese, by then. Being overweight is a big risk factor for cardiovascular disease and diabetes.

CUBAN FOOD-LIBRÉ

I met Marco, from Cuba, on an island in the Atlantic Ocean, near Africa.

IN CUBA, THERE is no such thing that the people there dislike Americans or America in any way. No one in Cuba would teach their kids something like that! But, what we have learned is that something must be wrong there; I'm talking about all the unnatural food that they are eating in America. In Cuba, we don't have any international restaurant chains, like McDonalds, that serve up food that destroys people's health and makes them fat. Actually, we don't have food from outside of Cuba. Everything we eat comes from nature—the meat, the tomatoes, everything. There are no extra, artificial ingredients in our food. I really hope that America returns to basic, natural, organic food, so people can live without all the suffering that comes with their modern food.

DID YOU KNOW

Approximately two billion of the world's population is overweight, and that number is increasing quickly?

"Something must be wrong! Americans have more fitness centers than any other country in the world, yet, at the same time, they just keep getting fatter than anyone else."

Josefina, Bolivia

"I've seen many Americans eat without using a knife and fork properly, especially in fast food restaurants. It seems like using these tools takes too long for them to get the food into their mouth, so they choose to use their hands and, instead, throw the food into their mouths. What happened to enjoying a meal, nice and slowly? I think this reflects all of American society—it's very stressful and unhealthy."

Vanessa, France

 DID YOU KNOW

One out of every five children in America is overweight?

"Americans eat pancakes and syrup for breakfast and wonder why they are fat! I never eat breakfast in America due to the lack of real, natural food."

Karen, Australia

DEADLY AMERICAN ADVICE

Ron Rosedale is an internationally-known expert in nutritional and metabolic medicine. He truly believes that Americans need to change their way of eating.

THE MAIN REASON that Americans are getting sicker and fatter every year is that they listened to their doctor and other medical professionals and followed their advice. We follow a high-carbohydrate diet. We have been told to eat as low-fat as possible. Since we have started to do that, we have gotten sicker and sicker.

That single piece of advice, to eat a low-fat, high-carbohydrate diet, has probably killed more Americans than any other single event in human history. I can't even imagine how many people have died due to that ridiculous advice, which is based on no science whatsoever. In fact, it is probably based more on politics, or what I call "kindergarten medicine". We have been taught that

eating fat makes us fat, but that's not how the body works. We must stop listening to the medical professionals who have given us deadly advice over the last half century.

The health situation in America is extremely serious—actually much more serious than people realize; both from a health standpoint and an economic standpoint. When we have to take care of all the sick people, it's going to really stress the economy of just about every nation in the world.

The food we are told to eat, high in carbohydrates and whole grains, gives us metabolic chaos in the body. It turns to sugar.

Our biggest problem is changing the minds of the medical professionals that are being led by large corporations. Right now, major agriculture companies, the ones that are selling carbohydrates and sugars, support a lot of the politics and a lot of the medicine and false information.

One of the things that most needs to change is the way medical studies are published. The vast majority, well above 75 percent, of medical studies that are published have nothing at all to do with science, but are related to marketing efforts, instead of health. Right now, science isn't science any longer—it's big business.

Medicine today is being controlled by large corporations, whose objective is to maximize profit and not maximize health. That really underlies the major reasons for the huge upswing in the chronic diseases of aging. Unless we get to the root of that, nothing's going to change.

Exercise is being overemphasized as a solution for obesity, albeit a small solution. We have more health clubs in the U.S., by far, than any other nation on earth. But it is my experience that it doesn't matter how hard you exercise, if you are not eating properly. The reality is that people aren't eating properly. They can't compensate how poorly they are eating with enough exercise to become healthy. One thing we do know—what we've been doing is wrong, totally wrong! If we continue to eat as we are being told to, we're just going to get worse and worse. We know for certain that a high-carbohydrate diet makes us worse off, and causes diseases. There is so much science to back up that statement, and it's not even new science—it goes back to when I was at medical school.

The medical profession really needs to take a long, hard look in the mirror and say, "We have been giving out the wrong information and we have been killing people for half a century. We need to change." Until they can do that, there won't be a change.

The good news for Americans who want to change their lives for the better is that the human body is incredibly resilient. It's never too late to make a change. Even for the worst people, it takes only three to four weeks to see great results, and if you're not that bad, it might only take a week.

It's amazing to me when I see people who have had diabetes for forty years, and even though they have been treating it with an incredible number of medications, we have been able to totally take them off medication and one hundred percent reverse their diabetes. I'm not talking about improving the diabetes; I'm saying we got rid of the diabetes completely. Obesity is easy to reverse. The best advice I can give is to eat a very low-carbohydrate, high-fat and moderate-protein diet. That alone can reverse diabetes, obesity and even cancer, to many extents. Eat a diet that keeps your lepton and insulin levels low, because that's really, really critical. The carbohydrates can be divided into fiber, or not fiber. Any carbohydrate that is not fiber will turn into sugar.

The healthiest food you can eat is fat—it doesn't raise lepton, glucose or insulin. Fat is the cleanest fuel to burn. Examples of good fats to eat include avocado, coconut oil, butter, olives and olive oil.

Most people think that they are being very healthy, but they have been led right over a cliff by what they have been taught. That needs to change because what Americans eat is just horrible. If we eat the opposite of what we have been taught, we will do a lot better. If you eat exactly as you have been taught by medical professionals, it would be extremely dangerous. That what's really scary! Right now, people are making an attempt to be healthy, and they think the reason they are sick is because they are not doing what they're told. It's the other way around—the reasons why they are so sick is because they are mostly doing what they were told. Americans have gotten sicker because they have been listening.

1.   My advice to Americans who want to change in order to live a better and longer life is: Don't listen to the doctor. I hate to say it, but it's true. Anything that has to do with chronic disease and nutrition, don't listen to your doctor. Chances are that he or she will give you the opposite advice of what makes you healthy.

2.   Eat properly. What properly means is don't eat food that turns to sugar—that's really critical. Don't be afraid of eating fat. Don't go after carbohydrates and especially avoid no-fiber carbohydrates that just turn to sugar. You can live perfectly well without carbohydrates, even though it is impossible to avoid them completely.

Americans have very little idea about what is causing their poor health situation. They're being brainwashed into thinking that they need to do more of what they are taught. It's not that the information doesn't reach the people; it's that the information is totally wrong in the first place. I don't think it's the fault of the American people, I think it's the doctors' fault because right now, doctors are being controlled by the pharmaceutical industry. They make money off of sick people. Getting the right information from the doctors has to change—we just have to get the truth out there, and also to the rest of the world. Unfortunately, the world follows America, especially when it comes to health care. We're leading people over a cliff, so don't follow us. Where we, Americans, are going right now is not a good place to be.

Very few physicians have had such consistent success in helping diabetics to eliminate or reduce their need for insulin and to reduce heart disease without drugs or surgery. Dr. Ron Rosedale is the founder of the Rosedale Center, co-founder of the Colorado Center for Metabolic Medicine (Boulder, Colorado) and founder of the Carolina Center of Metabolic Medicine (Asheville, North Carolina). Through these centers, he has helped thousands, suffering from so-called incurable diseases, to regain their health. One of Dr. Rosedale's life goals is to wipe out Type II diabetes in the USA, as a model for the rest of the world.

"I like the Americans I meet in Europe, but I'm not sure I feel the same about Americans in America. They are different—how should I say it—more old-minded."

Ernst, Germany

"It's not necessarily the Americans themselves that attract me, but their way of thinking, and how they actually live their lives."

Yelena, Georgia

"American credit card companies must just love these big-spending American customers."

Kathy, Ireland

A FOREIGNER IN AMERICA

Anne-Marie Kuhlman, originally from Stockholm, Sweden, has lived in America for over fifteen years. She now lives in Northern California, and previously lived in Oregon and Hawaii. On a daily basis, she shares about her experience of moving to America on her blog.

THE FIRST THING I noticed when I came to America is how much more space there was for individuality, and that is something I still feel is significant and that I appreciate a lot. In Sweden, we must always be careful not to stand out from the "normal" crowd. To fit into "the group" there is much more important than individualism. In America, they respect individuality, and that just feels so good.

In Scandinavia, we have something called "Every Man Rights" which means that people can walk everywhere in nature and close to the seaside without obstacles. It means that no one owns the land between a house and the sea, that everyone can move freely there. Here in the U.S., I really miss the Every Man Rights because I often find signs that say: "Keep out," "No Trespassing" and "Private Property," and they stop me from enjoying the beauties of nature.

Other things in America that deserve to be changed are Americans' lack of knowledge about other parts of the world, and all of the violence that sometimes seems built-in to the American society and mentality.

But, in general, I'm satisfied with America, even though I miss small things like Swedish food. But when I'm in Sweden, what I really miss about the USA is all the organic food you can find in America that doesn't exist in my former home country. I also miss the openness and politeness between people that I have become accustomed to here in America.

What people from other countries should really learn from Americans is how they like to be themselves—we should learn to be more open and dare to just be ourselves. We should get rid of the shyness—that doesn't exist in the U.S.—and step out of the crowd and not be so damned serious all the time.

People in America are great small-talkers to people they haven't met before, and that feels more human to me.

But, I also think it's harder to form friendships here in America as compared to Sweden, though that must seem like a paradox. Once you overcome the Swedish shyness, it's easy to make friends there. In the USA, you talk to everyone no matter what, but after that, it's difficult to gain deeper friendship. Even Americans say they agree with me on that.

I've also noticed that Americans are more respectful to older people. Where I come from, older people aren't worth much, but in America, older people are valuable.

A lot of things in America are gigantic! The roads, fruits, vegetables, cars, trees and everything else are just a lot bigger than other places in the world! But, I don't know if Americans themselves are aware of that since most of them haven't been outside of the American borders.

Americans believe in themselves and that is why they become good at sports, music, dancing and a whole lot else. Others don't have the faith in themselves that Americans do, and because of that, they create hurdles for themselves.

I don't think Americans and people who live outside of America view America in the same way, and I don't believe Americans would recognize themselves in the way outside people look at them. Americans really don't understand that people find them loud and noisy, and that we can hear them everywhere. They just talk louder in America, that's how they are, and they also "project" their voices much more when they have something to say. Foreigners think that Americans could be more humble.

To leave your home country and move to America requires huge restructuring. The USA has a monotonous everyday life, like all other countries in the world, and to live here is absolutely not a "Hollywood" life, as many people from other parts of the world believe. It took me years to accept the way of life here in America. The culture differences are so much bigger than you could even imagine.

And what you must learn, but what's almost impossible to learn, is how to handle all the unwritten laws in the American culture—unwritten laws that you can only learn if you actually grow up in America.

"What a burden the American girls must carry that they must lose their virginity before a certain age! If they wait, they're considered strange or abnormal."

Judith, Austria

The American language is not sophisticated, and neither are the people."

Kate, Malta

"American girls seem either very liberated, or very prude. It's very rare to find something in between."

Nisha, India

FROM THE DOWNTON ABBEY

Here are some thoughts from Elizabeth McGovern, an actress in the BBC television show, Downton Abbey, who moved from America to live in the U.K.

ABOUT LACK OF DISCIPLINE:

There are so few rituals in America today. Anything goes. There's so much mobility, and anything is possible day and night. In America, you can do anything 24/7. I think people would like to have that kind of discipline they see in *Downton Abbey*.

ABOUT MOVING TO BRITAIN:

It wasn't easy to move there; I spent twenty years rehearsing the part of an American living in Britain, and I still haven't quite figured out how to do it.

Here is an example: an American will say, "I quite like something." That means that they like it, that they really like it. A Brit will say, "I quite like something." But, that means that they don't like it at all. Americans say what they think, literally.

MAESTRO

"Americans have very odd taste in music, especially when it comes to new music. To me, modern American pop music is just noise. For example, it's difficult for me to understand all the hip-hop they listen to there—a music genre almost without melodies and with ridiculously shallow lyrics. Older American music is more sincere and quite good. Nowadays, American country music is absolutely the best Americans have to offer.

Luicia, Columbia

DID YOU KNOW
The piano is the most popular instrument in the United States? Around twenty-one million Americans play the piano.

"If anyone has wondered where the best musicians in the world are, go to America. Even the smallest bar has top musicians who really know their craft."

Aleks, violinist from Turkey

THREE PEOPLE IN DUBAI, UNITED ARAB EMIRATES

1) *"Why is absolutely everything such a big competition for Americans? You know, sometimes winning is worse than losing. You may have won the battle against your neighbor, but then again you will always have a bad relationship with him."*

Hussein, United Arab Emirates

2) *"I have always liked America, but the development there is really going in the wrong direction. Before, America had proud cowboys and Indians. Now, they have hip-hoppers and alcoholics."*

Rami, United Arab Emirates

3) *"I don't think Americans dress themselves properly. It seems like many Americans spend more money on their pets than they do on themselves, or even their own kids."*

Gurjot, India

THE UNITED STATES OF AMERICA

Population: 319,000,000

Area: 3,531,905,43 square miles

Capitol city: Washington, D.C.

President: Barack Obama

Currency: U.S. dollar (USD)

Independence day: Fourth of July

Location:
North America, bordering both the North Atlantic Ocean and the North Pacific Ocean, between Canada and Mexico

Main industries:
Petroleum, motor vehicles, aerospace, steel, telecommunications, electronics, food processing, chemicals, consumer goods, mining, lumbering

Colors of American flag: Red, white and blue

Citizenship:
With very few exceptions, persons who are born in the United States become American citizens regardless of their ethnic background or of the citizenship and national origins of their parents. In this

respect, the United States differs from many other countries that do not automatically confer citizenship on persons merely on the basis of birth within their national jurisdictions. Open acceptance has characterized the American nationality process since the nation's founding, despite changes to laws and regulations over the years.

Population density: About thirty-two persons per square kilometer

Life expectancy at birth for Americans born in 2006:
White males: 73.8 years; white females: 79.6 years; non-white males: 68.9 years; non-white females: 76.1 years

Monaco is number one on the list of life expectancy by country, with an average of 89.68 years for males and females combined. America is number 50 on the life expectancy list.

In 2011, life expectancy at birth for the entire U.S. population was 78.7 years. Life expectancy for the Hispanic population within the U.S. was 81.4 years in 2011. Hispanic females had the highest life expectancy at birth (83.7 years), followed by non-Hispanic white females (81.1 years).

States in the southeast region of the U.S. has lower life expectancy than those in other regions of the country.

Population by gender:
Females 50.8%
Males 49.2%

Population by age:
5-17 years: 17.4%
18-44 years: 37.2%
45-64 years: 25.2%
65 years and over: 14.1%

Number of people age 65 or older:
  1967: 19.1 million
  2005: 36.8 million
  2010: 40.3 million

In the U.S., the population of seniors is expected to grow by slightly more than double, from about 41 million to 86 million by 2050.

Population by race:
  White: 72.4%; in 2004: 80.4%
  Hispanic or Latino origin: 16.3%
  Black: 12.6%; in 2004: 12.4%
  Asians: 4.8%
  American Indian, Alaska native persons: 0.9%
  Native Hawaiian and Other Pacific Islander: 0.2%

Health care:
84.5% of the U.S. population is covered by private or government health insurance. There are 254 physicians for every hundred thousand people, 5,890 hospitals, 3.6 beds for every one thousand people and 39.1 million people covered by Medicare, a health insurance program provided by the federal government primarily for people age 65 and older.

Immigrant population:
  Legal immigrants in the U.S. in 2012: 46 million; in 2000: 31 million
  Illegal immigrants: estimated to be between 6 million and 9 million currently residing in the United States.

Visitors to the United States:

48 million international visitors in 2006; 67 million visitors in 2012

Education:

Percentage of the population age 25 or older who earned at least a high school diploma: 51% in 1967; 85% in 2005

Number of single Americans: 100 million

Jobs:

Americans work in a wide variety of occupations. Here are some samples:

Gaming services workers (gambling): 98,000

Hairdressers and cosmetologists: 738,000

Chefs and head cooks: 317,000

Firefighters: 243,000

Musicians, singers, related workers: 213,000

Bakers: 183,000

Taxi drivers and chauffeurs: 291,000

Service station attendants: 100,000

Farmers and ranchers: 827,000

Pharmacists: 248,000

Teachers: 6,800,000

Top five religious denominations in the United States:

1. Roman Catholic Church, 69 million
2. Southern Baptist Convention, 16.3 million
3. United Methodist Church, 8 million
4. Mormon Church (Jesus Christ of Latter Day Saints), 5.6 million
5. Church of God in Christ, 5.5 million

 ## SIX FROM THE CRADLE OF WESTERN CIVILIZATION

1) *"If Americans are so concerned about how people view them, why don't they do something about it?"*

Spiros, Athens, Greece

2) *"I have to be honest—the most terrible guests we have here are from Israel. Germans and Russians are also very difficult customers. When it comes to rating the best guests, we actually find Americans at the top of the list. They can behave, they smile and they talk to us with equal respect."*

Nikki, works in a Greek restaurant on
the island of Rhodes, Greece

3) *"I have always assumed that Americans were weird and strange, but I had a totally wrong impression. Most of them are actually very cool, and they are certainly fun to hang out with."*

Evy, works in a hotel in Rhodes, Greece

4) *"The distance between everything in America is so, extremely huge. Sometimes it takes a two-hour drive to find a place to buy a burger."*

Cristos, Crete, Greece

5) *"Americans like the old saying: 'Good fences make good neighbors.'"*

Andreas, Crete, Greece

6) *"Not many Americans understand why so many of them are so arrogant."*

Georgos, Athens, Greece

AT THE THERAPIST'S OFFICE

AMERICANS' COMMITMENT ISSUES are usually related to their fear of making a bad choice for the future. What if this isn't the "right" person for me? What if something changes? (And it will!) Certainly, in American culture, there are a lot of myths about having to find the "right" person in order to "live happily ever after."

We, as Americans, put communication high on the list of desirable attributes of a marriage; yet, few of us have any real training in communication. A corollary to this is the expectation that I can read your mind, or that you can read mine.

As society changes, of course, the family changes along with it. In the 1950s, American families considered themselves successful so long as everyone played their individual roles well: Mother stayed home and took care of the house and raised the children, Father went to work and "brought home the bacon." These days, following the so-called "sexual revolution" and the women's movement, those traditional role expectations don't fly. Now, we're looking for intimacy and joy.

Before, American families were geographically closer together, which gave family members more of a sense of safety and belonging. But if someone moved away, you probably did not expect to see them again! I think of the Conestoga wagons heading west. We all want to feel safe, but we also want passion and adventure. And we have a relatively new expectation that we can be "happy," since it's tempting to blame the other for one's problems, rather than looking into oneself.

The reason why America has such a high divorce rate is that we can afford it, for one thing. When a family lives a hardscrabble life, they're not about to give up the security provided by a partner, even if they don't like each other anymore. Also, the fact that divorce has become common makes it even more likely to be viewed as a solution to marriage troubles—we tend to do what our parents did, or what our friends do. There's very little societal criticism of divorce. Often, the children pay the price, though. The effect on the children makes a case for not taking either divorce or remarriage as lightly as some people do. We need to become a lot more aware of the emotional price of divorce that occurs in the absence of a societal norm that holds families sacred.

Fifty years ago, I'd say most families believed punishment was the best way to raise their children. Now, that concept has been pretty much turned upside down. As with any extreme, a parent can be too encouraging. "Good job!" is better saved for real accomplishment; used indiscriminately it loses all meaning. But, I want parents to be wise, which is a pretty hard assignment for young parents who have had no training except their own childhoods. We tend to either do what our parents did, or try to do the opposite, which is likely to have the same effect.

Probably the most common sexual problem in America is a lack of desire. People can love each other deeply and be uninterested in one another sexually.

We all want to feel safe, but for passion to arise, there has to be some risk.

What I do see these days, is that people are much more willing to talk about and ask for help with their sex lives than, say, fifty years ago.

In both American society and relationships, I would like to see less "right/wrong split," and more "both/and thinking." "Right/wrong" is a trap that no one can get out of because everyone wants to be the "right" one. "Both/and" gives us room for collegiality and growth.

The thing that concerns me, even though I quite enjoy the technology I use, is the rise of "connecting" through only mechanical means. Our brains are built for face-to-face connection, and even Skype, as handy as it is, doesn't accomplish that. One of my all-time favorite quotes is from a book called *A General Theory of Love* by Thomas Lewis: "The signature lesson of the twentieth century is that unforeseen complications are ever the faithful companions of technological progress. The convenient devices that enable extensive mobility are problematic because limbic regulation operates weakly at a distance. We have the means to establish a peripatetic lifestyle, but we will never have the brains for it."

Spending more time with new technology is a challenge for American relationships. The fact is, in order to prosper as human beings (meaning to prosper relationally, not in a financial sense), we need real face time with one another. Neuro-imaging clearly shows changes in the brain relating to personal interaction. A person in pain actually feels less pain when a loved one is close. Brain scans show a mother's brain and a baby's brain operating in harmony (this is part of how a mother knows what her baby needs). We regulate each other when we're in physical proximity. I can calm a panicked patient by regulating my own emotional arousal. Did you ever notice how, in an argument, voices go up, and up, and up and never down? That's a destructive feedback loop in action. Next time you find yourself in an argument, try to purposely lower your voice—you may have a surprising experience.

Stability means finding people who regulate you well and staying near them. The study of attachment is very big these days. Someone said, "Attachment [to others] isn't just a good idea, it's the law!" One idea that demonstrates our human need of attachment is the study of children hospitalized in sterile conditions, not allowed visits from outside relatives in order to avoid contagion. These ill children are even kept in isolation boxes, so as not to be touched by potentially dirty hands. Statistically, the isolated children got sicker, often from the diseases they were supposed to be protected against. Human contact is vital.

During the Middle Ages, the worst thing that could happen to someone was to be "ex-communicated," literally, taken out of communication with others. It was a death-sentence because one cannot survive with no human contact.

So, is Facebook making Americans lonely? Of course, the answer is no—we make ourselves lonely by the way we use Facebook. The problem with Facebook, and other networking sites, is that they are a poor substitute for the real thing.

I've noticed that so-called "diet" foods, especially things like diet sodas, actually increase hunger. When you fool the taste buds, such as with artificial sweetener, the body expects to get something needed. When it doesn't, hunger increases. It's the same with junk foods—when you don't get the nutrients you need, you want more, more, more of everything in front of you, which continues to starve the body with a sea of empty calories.

The same can be said for "social networking". You can have a million Facebook friends and still be starved for real relationships.

Increasing your Facebook friend count gives a momentary illusion of relationships, followed by an increase in longing for the real thing. One of the problems here, as with food, is the experience in the moment that you're getting something you need, even as you starve.

Possibly the biggest enemy to Americans' sex life is expectations. Americans want the safety of reliable relationships, but the excitement of risk. Everybody wants to feel safe, but real intimacy is all about taking the risk of being vulnerable (literally, open to harm). Enter distractions: TV, the Internet, overworking and even fighting.

Good sex is about two individuals taking the risk of exploring the space between them, being excited by their differences, being able to be entirely present, in themselves while with the other.

Unfortunately, our ideal couples are, more or less, joined at the hip, never argue and are always "nice" to each other. Safe, but not sexy!

Let's face it—using new technology correctly means turning it off and looking your friend or your partner directly in the eyes, an eye-to-eye, *and* an "I-to-I" relationship. Social media is fun and a great icebreaker. Like texting on the phone, it's a convenient way to plan a get-together. But, the get-together has to happen. I find it tragic to see kids clustered together, all looking at their phones as they text—each other! Social media is good for letting a lot of people know your big news and it's great for continuing contacts that might otherwise be lost.

Cheryl Gerson is a licensed therapist for individuals, couples and groups in New York City, New York, USA

"Loneliness seems to have become the great American disease."

John Corry, politician, Ireland

"It seems really important for Americans to own the newest and coolest technical devices, like iPads and smartphones, but what's even more important is that others must see that they have them."

Grace, Northern Ireland

"I have always wondered where the Americans got the idea to grill the marshmallows, but then, come to think of it, they put whatever there is on a barbecue, don't they?"

Stig, Sweden

"Many American men don't accept the reality that they're not as irresistible as they think they are."

Ana Dora, Spain

SHIP AHOY!

Masha Maria, from Slovenia, has met a huge number of people during her travels around the world. She has worked on several cruise ships, across the Seven Seas, as well as lived in the USA, Canada, Czech Republic and Slovenia.

WHEN I AM not in the United States, I really miss it. I miss the kindness I find there and the way they are open to other people. I never find my inner self in Slovenia, where I am from. There are some negative facts about Slovenians and Europeans: they're not so open to things, and their jealousy and envy goes beyond normal. In the U.S., no one is judged by whatever his or her line of work is or how they look, and that's why I love to live in the United States, where people can be whoever they want to be. I will say that only a small percentage of the European population is very open, kind and talkative. Europeans are the opposite of what Americans are. I have worked with about sixty different nationalities, and I can tell that the Americans are among the most kind and friendly ones. They know how to make you smile.

Americans also like to dance! Actually, I think Americans must have dance blood in their veins because they just know how to move to any kind of music. They like to have fun and are never shy; even guys who don't know the dance steps dance eagerly in America.

I have dated American men and I have to say that they are very relaxed and open-minded. People say that you can't find these kinds of nice men in the world anymore. But in fact, Americans are just that nice.

America is just so different in many ways, but to really understand what's good about the country, I advise people to go there and stay for awhile.

What I find a bit over-the-top, though, are all the Americans in their baseball and sports clothes, with their favorite team and player on them. Many Americans seem to live only for that specific team, or that specific match, and that seems a bit weird to me.

When it comes to food, my admiration for America stops. I don't like American food at all, except for maybe some donuts and Starbucks coffee. I am very picky when it comes to food, and I have to say that we are lucky, back in Europe, to have such good, healthy, quality food. In the United States, I had a hard time finding tasty, fresh and healthy food. When I arrived to the States for the first time, in 2007, I was actually shocked. I thought that people were eating unhealthy food only in the movies, but I was totally wrong. Now I understand why so many American people have diabetes and serious diseases. I think Americans must increase their knowledge about what is healthy food and what is not.

Speaking of knowledge, I must say that Europeans are very knowledgeable and educated as compared to Americans.

Another thing that shocked me was when I learned about the typical mother's maternity leave in the U.S. What I learned, when I stayed with my friend in Virginia, is that the maternity leave is only three months, depending on which state you are from, and, unlike Europe, mothers usually don't get paid for maternity leave. In my country we get paid for nine months of maternity leave, and in other countries it goes up to twelve months of paid leave. We also aren't paying for all the necessary doctors during pregnancy, that's included in our national health care.

MOTHER, MOTHER

THE STATE OF the World's Mothers report in 2012, by Save the Children Foundation, examines the well-being of mothers and their children in 165 countries. Based on measures like infant mortality, mothers' education and breastfeeding rates, they have ranked the best and the worst countries for moms. Here are the results:

1) Norway (best)
2) Iceland
3) Sweden
4) New Zealand
7) Australia
10) United Kingdom/Netherlands
14) France
19) Canada
21) Italy
25) USA
163) Yemen
164) Afghanistan
165) Niger (worst)

Norway tops the list with one of the most generous maternity leave policies in the developed world.

When it comes to USA's ranking, they are considered low and rate quite poorly on a number of measures, such as:

- **Risk of dying from childbirth:** Mothers in the USA face the highest risk of maternal death of any industrialized nation.

- **Maternity leave:** Maternity leave policies in the USA are among the least generous of any wealthy nation. It is the only developed country, and one of only a handful of countries in the world, that does not guarantee paid leave for working mothers.

"Americans grow old with respect and admiration— not with all the age discrimination that we have back home."

Peter, Sweden

"An American sailorman in uniform is any girl's dream."

Elena, Greece

"I think that Americans, at an early age, learn that second best is like losing."

Phueng, Thailand

PELEKAS NEWS

People from different cultures and from all over the world have visited the Alexandros restaurant and apartments in the village of Pelekas on the Greek island of Corfu. The manager, Alex Vergis, has formed his own thoughts about how the American people conduct themselves.

THE AMERICAN GUYS that came to the village of Pelekas were, actually, a bit afraid of other people. But thanks to the friendly Swedish girls, they changed their minds very easily while they were here.

I believe that Americans are more innocent and naive than Europeans. It is a lot easier to fool an American, to tell him a story and make him believe it is true, than to fool someone else.

But American girls were very suspicious when it came to the local boys. The local boys found it very difficult to take American girls to bed, but, at the same time, it was always easy to get a blowjob.

Americans can be impulsive. When they are here, the plan is often to stay a day, or two, but often, they like it here so much that they spend more than a week.

Americans love all the local foods of the countries they visit. Here in Greece, they ate dishes like Greek salad, moussaka, baklava and retsina wine, and they made sure they finished their plates every single time. Americans were very big spenders in Pelekas. They were also friendly and generous. I even got a lot of invitations to visit America, to come and stay there—often for free. One example is a girl who worked for an airline company in America that offered to fly me over there for free if I would come to visit her in New York.

Americans are very polite and similar to Scandinavians. In my opinion, the nicest people in the world are the Swedes and the Norwegians, and the strange thing is that Americans are always getting along so well with these Scandinavians. They are eating, drinking and going clubbing together.

American boys and girls are very loud when they're drinking, and Americans drink quite a lot, but can never beat the Scandinavian Vikings! Americans are not violent when they drink, and that's a very good thing.

Americans have changed lately. In the past, they were more open to other cultures. Unfortunately, Americans tend to listen to their own music now, rather than some foreign band. In the 80s and 90s, Americans looked like normal guys and acted like other young European students. Now, they don't do that anymore; they have actually turned very strange compared to the rest of the world.

What I find very odd about Americans is that they are not as well-educated as they should be, not only about their own country, but also about Europe and the rest of the world. Europeans tend to know more about America than Americans do.

"Americans don't just sit inside and wait for success to happen—they march out the doorstep and find it by themselves."

Lyuba, Ukraine

FIVE AMERICANS ON MANHATTAN, NEW YORK

1) *"The major difference between us and the rest of the world is that we stand up for what we believe in."*

Steve, USA

2) *"We Americans are very dramatic; every little thing has a tendency to be so giant for us."*

Rachel, USA

3) *"I'm a very, very rare American. I eat when I'm hungry and stop when I'm full."*

Guillaume, USA

4) *"Americans are so predictable; we really like to know what's around the next corner, and that limits us to live the life we want to live."*

Laura, USA

5) *"People say that America has come so far, but really, how far have we come? In my opinion, we're moving backwards—fast."*

Matt, USA

 "The biggest criticizer of America I have ever met is an American."

Aidan, Ireland

FIVE FOREIGNERS ON MANHATTAN, NEW YORK

1) *"I have noticed that Americans make rectangular cakes, while we make them round."*

Noelle, France

2) *"Many Americans look like old Barbie dolls after all their plastic surgery. It's not pleasant to look at and it makes people, like me, very uncomfortable."*

Veronique, Tunisia

3) *"I applaud Americans because they applaud each other.*

Natalia, Netherlands

4) *"I have never met a shy American, and compared to the rest of the world, that's a huge advantage for Americans.*

Leon, France

5) *"Baseball is bit of a girly game, isn't it?"*

Robert, Austria

THANK YOU

SO MANY PEOPLE are false and fake when they criticize America. Just think about what Americans have done in the past to make this world a little bit better:

- Making good movies (not everyone does that)
- Recording great music
- Creating the Internet and websites
- Sharing their art and literature
- Producing television, video games and entertainment
- Inventing phones and other revolutionary technology
- Providing protection and supplies in both war and peace

Americans have brought more peace and justice to this world than anyone else, even with their own lives at stake. Who else will do that for you? Nobody. And what exactly are we doing, ourselves, to make this world a better place? Think about that! There is only one thing that is proper for all of us to say to the Americans: Thank you!

Fateh, India

AMERICANS IN MEXICO

AMERICANS ARE GREAT. They do not just look for a relaxing day on the beach, something must take place. They are always looking to participate in some activities when they are on holiday. We have students, instructors and guests who come from everywhere around the world, but in the winter season we have mostly Americans. In general, I think kids from the USA already have too many things to care about, and not enough time for learning new sports—TV and video games are easier to learn. So, I would advise American parents to get their kids active much earlier than they do.

Americans also like to tip more than others, and, of course, we like that! Europeans ask for more discounts. However, Americans, in the last few years, also have tried to ask for more discounts.

Marco Cristofanelli,
owner of Extreme Control Kite Boarding in Tulum, Mexico

FIVE RANDOM PEOPLE IN MADRID, SPAIN

"Americans like to be friends, but only in a distant, superficial way."

Kristina, Spain

"It's no doubt that Americans love their country, but what surprises me is that they don't know why."

Javier, Spain

"Americans need heroes to look up to; that's why they have created them."

Felipe, Spain

"Americans don't take responsibility for what they are doing with their lives—that's what all the lawyers are for."

Janine, Spain

"Being both noisy and nosy is considered rude in most parts of the world, except for in America."

Nicola, Spain

HAPPY HOLIDAYS

Some holidays in America are:

Martin Luther King, Jr. Day - observed on the third Monday in January

Groundhog Day - observed on February 2nd, since 1887

Valentine's Day - observed on February 14th

Memorial Day - observed on the last Monday of May; Memorial Day originally honored the people killed in the American Civil War, but has become a day for remembering fallen Americans in all wars

Father's Day observed on the third Sunday of June; Father's Day, which celebrates all fathers in America, began in 1909 in Spokane, Washington, when a daughter requested a special day to honor her father, a Civil War veteran, who raised his children after his wife died

Independence Day – observed on July 4th; this federal holiday honors the nation's birthday

"On the Fourth of July, I feel like an American myself. It's like the world's national day for liberty."

Jimmy, Sweden

Labor Day – observed on the first Monday of September; honors the nation's working people, typically with parades; for most Americans it marks the end of the summer vacation season and the start of the school year

Columbus Day – observed on the second Monday in October

Halloween – observed on October 31st

Veterans Day – observed on November 11th

Thanksgiving - observed on the fourth Thursday in November; In the fall of 1621, the Pilgrims held a three-day feast to celebrate a bountiful harvest (many regard this event as the nation's first Thanksgiving); the Thanksgiving feast became a national tradition and almost always includes some of the foods served at the first feast: roast turkey, cranberry sauce, potatoes, and pumpkin pie

Pearl Harbor Remembrance Day – observed on December 7th

"It's wonderful with all of the celebration, but why the turkey every time?"
Lotte, Belgium

DID YOU KNOW

Americans also have enormous amounts of non-federal holidays to celebrate. Many of these holidays are quite bizarre: Serpent Day, Burning Snowman Day, Public Sleeping Day and these are only the tip of the iceberg?

"Americans really like to go all the way when it comes to celebrating their holidays."

Sophia, Canada

"More and bigger is better—I'm talking about how Americans celebrate their holidays."

Anne, Ireland

DID YOU KNOW?

There are even more holidays in America: Jews have their high holy days in September, Muslims celebrate Ramadan, African Americans celebrate Kwanzaa and Irish Americans celebrate St. Patrick's Day

"An American without a gun is a naked American."

Sarah, England

*"Americans accept any gender, age, size, nationality—
any person in the world! That's why I salute them."*

Irfan, Turkey

*"Americans don't have all these negative people that
tell you that everything is impossible."*

Rokas, Lithuania

THE LAW OF JANTE

"Stop talking nonsense!"

"Come down to the planet earth."

"That is absolutely impossible."

"No, no, no!"

In Norway, where I come from, sentences like that are common for kids to hear. Their parents, teachers and friends will instantly stop any childhood dream upon hearing something foolish like "I am special" or "I have a talent". This is because in my home country, everyone should be alike and no one should be better or different than another. When I was at my first feature-writing class as a journalism student, the first thing the teacher said to us was: "Don't any of you students think that you can write a book and work as an author. I have tried that and I know that it's not possible for any of you."

If we look under the surface, we see that it all comes down to jealousy and fear that others may have greater success than we might. In Norway, you don't want your friend or neighbor to have success—that would be the worst thing that could occur because you didn't achieve success as well. And because of that, if you try to achieve success, your friends and neighbors will start a campaign to do almost anything to put you down. If they haven't achieved the same success, why should you deserve it? They will talk behind they will continuously say that you lucky and they will never admit did something good. They will work against you because your successes are something they just can't stand. It doesn't matter what you have achieved or any form of success you have, they will tell you that it didn't come because of your talent, or all the work you put in. No, the reason for your success must be, to them, random luck because in Norway we must all be identical. Nobody there shall live in a bigger house than you, no one must be richer than their fellow citizen and no person should be happier than another. So, the most horrible thing that can happen to your friends and neighbors is when you achieve your well-deserved success! Then the cattle stand outside with their jealous eyes, thinking that your success is not fair to them because you are one of them, one of the crowd, one among the cattle.

As a result of your success, the head of the cattle must bring new weapons to the table so everyone can be equal again. It doesn't matter what the existing laws and rules are, they must now change. They must take you down somehow. One way the people of Norway react is to charge an extra tax to the newly rich guy, so he must give away his fortune to the state. Another way to stop individuals from blooming is to forbid private entities from starting a school for talented kids. This way, we can all be equal again and have the same joint purpose. We can all go the same direction, follow the same interests, work at the same office and live in the same types of apartments that cost exactly the same. We must, by all means, not stand out of the crowd or try to live our own lives because we risk being atypical and different than the rest of the crowd. That is the opposite of what the cattle in Scandinavia want. They don't want individuals; they don't want you to be proud of yourself! They want the cattle within their fences. Not even after blood, sweat and hard work, day and night for years to achieve your goals, will the stagnant cattle admit that you did well. It doesn't matter if you win the Olympic Games or find the cure for cancer, you will not be saluted by your neighbor and friends in Scandinavia because you are just one among the jealous cattle. Even stranger, they will never act like you are as good as them, even though you might be a lot better at something and have a wonderful life. That's just the way it is in Scandinavia, where equality has gone too far.

"The best revenge is massive success"

Frank Sinatra

In Norway, the small, everyday things work the same way as success. We don't easily give compliments to each other and we never tell others that they are smarter than us, even if they are. It's really a big mystery that we behave this way because it doesn't benefit anyone; it's just very sad.

I want to speculate on why we are this way, but a behavior like this is, to me, a clear sign of weakness and insecurity, and we Scandinavians have, sadly, been like this forever.

People who are confident and strong don't put random people and close friends down like we do; they lift each other up and appreciate them all the way to the finish line—success or not! The Danish-born writer, Aksel Sandemose, who later moved to Norway to become an author, struggled with the same issues. In his book, *A Fugitive Crosses His Tracks*, from 1933, he brought the "Law of Jante" to life. This law includes ten rules that are still significant today for the Scandinavian countries: Denmark, Sweden and Norway.

THE LAW OF JANTE:

1. You're not to think *you* are anything special.
2. You're not to think *you* are as good as *us*.
3. You're not to think *you* are smarter than *us*.
4. You're not to convince yourself that *you* are better than *us*.
5. You're not to think *you* know more than *us*.
6. You're not to think *you* are more important than *us*.
7. You're not to think *you* are good at anything.
8. You're not to laugh at *us*.
9. You're not to think anyone cares about *you*.
10. You're not to think *you* can teach *us* anything.

THE NEW LAW

I still believe in the American dream. America has always been a country for underdogs, where David beats Goliath, where dyslexics write books, where the poor guy from a bad neighborhood gets fame and fortune. I

love that underdog philosophy. We all have seen it happen and it still happens: an American company can grow enormously in just a few weeks, you can become one of the most popular artists in the world overnight and a family can become financially safe very quickly. All of those things are okay in the U.S., and why shouldn't they be? The Americans salute and support their own people when they achieve success.

It's time to bury the ridiculous Law of Jante. We need new

laws that can be relevant for the whole world. But, to be honest, we have too many stupid unwritten rules in the world as it is! Let's value individuals and freedom. Let's greet our brothers and let all people be who they want to be, instead of shaping them into something they don't want to be. And everyone needs to know, no matter what background they have, that they can have high goals and accomplish a better life, as well as fame and fortune, if they aim for it and work hard enough. That is what the American dream is all about—a better life.

People must also know that others care for them and love them throughout their daily struggles. We must value the freedom of individual beliefs and ambitions. I don't believe that everyone is alike; I consider everyone different and special. We all have diverse talents to use so that we can live the life we want to live. The worst thing we can do to ourselves, and to human nature, is to choose the wrong path for our own life; the path everyone else is telling us to follow instead of what our heart says. Then, we will end up among the big cattle in Scandinavia—without purpose, ambitions and dreams of our own.

Only one country comes to my mind as the exact opposite of The Law of Jante—America. In America, everyone can make it, no matter who you are and where you come from. The American dream is not a fairytale; for many Americans, their vision has become a reality. Americans, even those who start with nothing, have "made it". To us outsiders, it seems that Americans don't have prejudiced thoughts about their fellow citizens, no matter their age, gender, color, nationality or background. Everyone is allowed to (and is encouraged to) take the golden ticket when it's within reach. That seems to be the spirit in the United States. People in America will support a friend, and they will cry with you along the way when you are facing hurdles and downturns, but they will not stop believing in you and they will approve of you, no matter what. They will even encourage you for whatever you are going for, whether it's an accomplishment on paper or an impossible task, because nothing is really unattainable in the American mind. At the same time, friends and family will show that they are pleased for you, not only after your reach your goal, but along the whole long road from the start. They will give you that extra energy you need when it seems like the whole world is turning against you, and when the day comes when you finally make it big, they will congratulate and celebrate you as much as if they had personally achieved success, too. In the minds of Americans there is a loyalty that says: "Stand by your friends and family—no matter what."

The American way of praising their friends is to involve everyone around them, to idolize their friends and make sure that everyone else knows that they are proud of that person. That kind of support is something that is very unusual outside of the American continent, but something I wish the whole world could be a part of. So, let's make a new world law where all people can be exactly who they are meant to be. Let's call it "The Law of Americans".

René Z

"I recently understood why Americans like Abba so much: 'Money, money, money' and 'The winner takes it all.'"

Calli, Mexico

"In retail stores in America, the sales staff treats us so incredibly well, as if we are their most important customer! Back home, the salesmen think we are there to irritate them."

Anders, Denmark

"I wonder how long Americans must wait until they reach the Promised Land."

Rika, Netherlands

"I believe that Americans who are so convinced that America is the greatest country in the world haven't tried something else."

Krista, Belarus

MOODS FROM THE SAHARA DESERT

IN MOROCCO, WE have many American visitors, and we always say that we find three types of them:

1. The quiet one
2. The outgoing one
3. The crazy one

The first one, **the quiet American,** is a bit brainwashed from the media. He is really afraid of us Moroccans in the beginning. I don't know what he has heard of us before he comes, but we feel the fear he has for us. After two to three days, he becomes more confident and feels safer, and he opens up a bit.

The **outgoing American** is like the typical American we all know. He talks and talks, and tells stories all the time. He is also a bit afraid in the beginning, but feels confident and safer after a few days.

The **crazy American** is often a traveler. He is the one who wants to explore everything that other people haven't experienced before. He is really not afraid of anything, and feels the kick of doing something new, something crazy or going to places not many others have been before. He has no fear at all.

So, in general, Americans get more confident after the first two or three days. After that, they treat us as best friends and start to spend a lot of money. Compared to other people in the world, Americans are among the kindest people we meet. They are certainly fun, pleasant to be with and very nice.

Benalila, Morocco, owns a Sahara adventure trip company in Africa

"While ordinary people try to avoid dangerous situations, Americans search for them."

Emanuel, South Africa

"I have met donkeys that are less arrogant and stubborn than Americans."

Natalia, Argentina

"All these Americans who constantly talk about how to get rich must have a really poor life."

Susanna, England

THE ECONOMIC WIND

"It really breaks my heart to see so many middle-class homeless people in America today—people that have not only lost their money, but also their dignity and hope for the future."

Knut, Norway

DID YOU KNOW?

In 2012, international travel and tourism spending reached a record $168 billion? It's up 10% from 2011 and increasing in 2013.

In 2012, there were 67 million international visitors to the United States. That's an increase of 4.3 million from the year before.

By 2017, the number of travelers from Brazil, China, and India—as compared to 2011—is expected to grow by 83%, 259%, and 47%, respectively. This represents a total of 4.4 million additional travelers just from these three countries by 2017. On average, each tourist that America attracts from these areas will spend $4,000 during their stay in the United States. The International Trade Administration has set a goal of

attracting over 100 million international visitors annually by 2021. These international visitors are projected to spend an estimated $250 billion per year, creating jobs and spurring economic growth in communities across the country.

Believing in the future is important to make the economy grow. A major problem in the USA is that homeowners have too much debt. This is because people spend money they don't actually have and because of the difference between their debt and their home's value, they can't sell their house, and consequently they can't move to find new jobs. That's how the real estate market becomes the glue in the American economy.

Robert J. Shiller, USA, Professor at Yale University

 DID YOU KNOW?

The average cost for tuition and fees at a private, non-profit, U.S. college in 1973 was $10,783 (adjusted for 2013 inflation). Costs have now tripled over the ensuing forty years, with the average tuition and fees total jumping to $30,094.

"We, in Europe, should be the first in line to help the economy in America, but unfortunately, many European countries need massive help, too."

Jozephine, Portugal

THE TOP 25 MOST PROSPEROUS NATIONS IN THE WORLD:

1. Norway
2. Denmark
3. Sweden
4. Australia
5. New Zealand
6. Canada
7. Finland
8. Netherlands
9. Switzerland
10. Ireland
11. Luxembourg
12. **U.S.** The U.S. has dropped out of the top ten for the first time, coming in at 12th.
13 - United Kingdom
14 - Germany
15 - Iceland
16 - Austria
17 - Belgium
18 - Hong Kong
19 - Singapore
20 - Taiwan
21 - France
22 - Japan
23 - Spain
24 - Slovenia
25 -   Malta

Source: Legatum Prosperity Index

 DID YOU KNOW

In America, the number of households with annual incomes of over one million dollars is expected to double before the year 2020?

DID YOU KNOW

Measuring from 2008-2012, 14.8% of Americans are living below the poverty level?

"A lot of American men don't take showers when they are out on a Saturday night. It's like a tornado of awful smells that hits you sometimes."

Yarah, Brazil

"Americans are the best actors in real life. I mean, they are really dramatic and always playing games with you; they are not to be trusted."

Louisa, Switzerland

 DID YOU KNOW

The global population is expected to increase by 38%, from 6.9 billion in 2010 to 9.6 billion in 2050?

FROM THE FAIRWAY

WHEN OUT SHOPPING in America, you always get help, a hello and a smile. In Norway, they don't even bother to look you in the eyes.

I believe Americans appreciate their jobs more. Even the cashier in a store values their job more than any of us. After all my traveling, I can say, for sure, that Americans are polite right through.

In the USA, they aren't afraid to tell you about their dreams. I think it's very wrong when you can't tell others what you wish for. Everybody must be allowed to have a dream.

In Norway, if I shared my dreams with others, they will use it against me if I don't succeed, and others will tell me: "You are so cocky," "You are so high [arrogant], you think you are the best." Why shouldn't I tell others about my goals? It's so typical for Norwegians to act like police.

I have never cared about what others say or think. I have the greatest expectations for myself, and I can't sit and listen to everyone who thinks they know everything better, because then I just would go nuts.

Suzann "Tutta" Pettersen, professional golfer, Norway

"Americans are so polite that it seems a little suspicious to me."

Alek, Albania

"Some Americans try to show their masculinity through big limousines, but it really has the opposite effect."

Annabel, South Africa

"Hollywood is the real 'Silicon Valley'."

Jana, Slovakia

WOOF WOOF

"It seems like most Americans have at least two dogs. What do they need the extra dog for?"

Andrew, New Zealand

"When I came to America, what I saw are people who wanted to train their dogs. They said that they wanted the dog to listen to them, but nobody was listening to the dog. Most of the time people wouldn't even walk the dog—a simple act of walking the dog. Many Americans have a big backyard so they want the dog to do everything in that backyard. The dog lives in a very beautiful jail, but lacks normal activity. Dogs in Mexico are skinny but don't have psychological problems. Dogs in America are chunky and they have psychological problems."

Dog whisperer Cesar Millan, Mexico

DID YOU KNOW?

If you own a Labrador retriever you are among many thousands of people. It's the most popular dog in America.

"Most of the girls I meet in other countries are quite honest and quite easy to understand. It's completely different with American girls who are like several people at the same time and so impossible to read. But that also makes them more interesting, more exciting."

Brett, Australia

"How come Americans still use all these dark wall-to-wall carpets in their rooms? Why use wall-to-wall carpets at all?"

Andrea, Switzerland

WHAT I HAVE LEARNED FROM AMERICANS

Jimlim is a public relations and marketing manager for the hotel company, JW Marriot in Thailand and Asia. She has lived in the USA, been all over Europe and worked and studied in countries like New Zealand, USA, France, Australia and Great Britain. She has also worked for the Travel Channel in Thailand.

I WAS LIVING IN South Carolina as an exchange student and it was totally different from what I was used to. For example, when we are at school in Asia, we are taught to follow and remember whatever is in the textbook, then to take the exam and get good scores. However, in the U.S., we are taught to think for ourselves. The result of that, later on, is that America has produced inventors and creative people. Nowadays, we see a lot of copies of American brands and goods in Asia, especially China, but you will find that the inventors and innovative people are from the western world and the USA. I think these products are related to how we were taught when we were young.

I like the American way of thinking and improving. Americans are innovative and think for themselves. They are more independent. In the USA, when people go to college, they are on their own once they leave home and have their own lives. In Asia, the kids may not leave their parents' home until they get married.

Asians should learn to be more on time and more effective in terms of working. The Thai are slower and need to be pushed to get things done. Asians could learn from Americans to work more effectively and handle things without force or micromanagement.

The morale of workers is not much different, but we treat others how we want to be treated. Sometimes there can be misunderstandings, but we will always resolve it if we communicate and use compassion. Americans should learn to be more patient and to be less confrontational. They should learn to be more sensitive and use different words so the listeners don't feel attacked when hearing their message.

While Americans think they know everything, in fact, most of the people in their country hardly get out of their comfort zone to explore the world. They are not open-minded enough to explore and accept different cultures. They think they are right and whoever thinks differently from them is wrong.

"In Asia, the entertainment could be sexy girls dancing on a bar pole or a lady boy show. In the USA, the entertainment is often television or a movie at the theater."

Jimlim, Thailand

When I was living in the USA, daily life revolved around God and Christianity. The Americans went to church every Wednesday and Sunday and they liked to be a part of Christianity and impose their religion upon everyone they met. They would say to me, directly, that if I didn't believe in God or Jesus, I would go to hell. So I always questioned myself, if God really loves me, would he burn me, a fifteen-year-old girl, in hell, just because I do not believe in Him? Anyway, I gave it a try and I started talking to God for certain issues, but I never got a reply from him, so I stopped.

When it comes to daily culture, Asia and the USA are completely different. America is focused on sports such as football and baseball. In Thailand, we have food culture—we love food. Food means love for us. If we share our food, we share our love. You can never go around hungry or run out of food in Thailand. People in the USA do not eat right. A lot of people are overweight and eat whatever the TV commercials show. They eat a lot of processed food. The food industry in the USA corrupted people and regulated something that benefits the economy rather than the people.

What people around the world may not know is that in the U.S., stores and restaurants have limited operating hours. In Bangkok, in Thailand, we have things going on 24/7. Bangkok is the true "City that never sleeps".

In Thailand, I was studying with only girls at school; there were no male students. As a result, I was very shy in front of guys and that wasn't a good starting point when I went to study in the outgoing USA. I still feel shy around guys, but I feel more comfortable now. I dated a boy when I was in the U.S.. He was very nice and a sporty person. He played baseball and I played softball and my host family coached us, so I got to see him every evening. We were friends from the start. I hardly say "I love you" to anyone and I never kissed him, though deep inside, I wish I did. Other American kids would kiss each soon after becoming girlfriend and boyfriend, but at that point in my life, I prevented myself from getting too close to the opposite sex. I believed that my first kiss would be on my wedding day when the priest asks me, "Would you accept this man to be your husband?" and then he would ask the man, "Would you accept this lady to be your wife?" and once we both agree, we'd then kiss. I imagine that that kiss would be my very first kiss. By dating this guy from the U.S., I came to realize that I feel attracted to men, and from that relationship, I learned that I should not wait to show my real feelings, that I should say "I love you" before it's too late.

I saw a lot of young kids get pregnant in the U.S.. It's quite common that people have sex there without being married, but my culture has taught that sex must be after marriage. However, as I've grown older, I have learned that life operates differently from what my family has taught me.

The Thai boys are shyer about approaching girls than the Americans. Even if they have been dating for a long time, abstaining from sex is not an issue. On the other hand, if you date foreign guys, it becomes an issue if you don't want to get intimate with him. I have a Thai friend who, at the age of twenty-eight, has been dating a guy for eight years, and they have never had sex. I would say that that must be quite rare in the U.S.

"Say 'I love you' before it's too late"

Jimlim, Thailand

THE JAILHOUSE BLUES PAGES

Through the years, there have been many weird laws instated in America. Here are some of them:

According to Illinois state law, it is illegal to speak English. The officially recognized language is "American."

In Jasper, Alabama, it is illegal for a husband to beat his wife with a stick larger in diameter than his thumb.

In Fairbanks, Alaska, it is illegal to feed alcoholic beverages to a moose.

In Tucson, Arizona, it is illegal for women to wear pants.

In Chicago, Illinois, it is illegal to fish in one's pajamas.

DID YOU KNOW?

The United States has the most prisoners in the world with over two million people in prison. That means that 715 of every 100,000 Americans are locked up. Number two on the list of most prisoners is China with about 1.5 million people in prison.

In Hartford, Connecticut, it's illegal to educate a dog.

In Florida, unmarried women who parachute on Sundays may be jailed.

In Idaho, boxes of candy given as romantic gifts must weigh more than 50 pounds.

In Chicago, Illinois, people who are diseased, maimed, mutilated or deformed to the point of being "an unsightly or disgusting object" are banned from going out in public.

In Kentucky, state law stipulates that a person is considered sober until he or she cannot hold onto the ground.

In Kentucky, it is illegal to remarry the same man four times.

In New Orleans, Louisiana, fire trucks are required by law to stop at all red lights.

In Portland, Maine, it is illegal for men to tickle women under the chin with feather dusters.

DID YOU KNOW?

A total of 7,225,800 people are either on probation, in prison or on parole in America.

In Baltimore, Maryland, it is illegal to wash or scrub sinks, no matter how dirty they get.

In Michigan, a state law stipulates that a woman's
hair legally belongs to her husband.

In Minnesota, women may face up to thirty days in
jail if they impersonate Santa Claus.

In Raton, New Mexico, it is illegal for a woman to ride a
horse down a public street wearing a kimono.

In Oregon, people who make "ugly faces" at dogs may be fined and/
or jailed.

In Morrisville, Pennsylvania, women need a permit to wear cosmetics.

In South Carolina, every citizen is obliged to carry his gun to church.

In South Dakota, it is illegal to lie down and fall asleep in a cheese
factory.

In Tennessee, it is illegal to use a lasso to catch a fish.

In Dyersburg, Tennessee, it is illegal for a woman to
call a man for a date.

In Vermont, women must obtain written permission
from their husbands to wear false teeth.

In St. Croix, Wisconsin, women are not allowed to wear anything
red in public

"America is an insane mixture of the very best and the very worst."

John Cleese, England, actor and comedian

"America has a beautiful, powerful and magic flag."

Elena, Russia

"Americans ask, 'How are you?' without caring; they don't even wait to hear the answer. Everybody is on autopilot."

Marek, Poland

ON AND OFF IN THE USA

T HROUGHOUT THE LAST thirty years, Swedish couple Viveca and Mats have been traveling in America. They have seen most of the continent, and they also write a blog about traveling in the USA.

When we're not in America, we miss being there, because we are always so happy when we are there. We experience so much more in America than anywhere else in the world. We have traveled almost all of the countries in Europe and the individual states in America are far more different from each other than the European countries are from one another. For example, there's more variation between California, the New England region, Florida and Ohio then there is among Spain, Italy and Greece. To be honest, the Americans are also friendlier than people from those European countries.

It's very easy to be a tourist in America. It's easy to get a hotel room, and they are cheap and good. What amazes us every time is that America is just like what we have predicted, exactly as we have seen on TV and in movies before we arrived. The country is just as beautiful as we expected it to be.

We really enjoyed the different states we have been to in America, with the exception of Florida, where everything is fake and plastic, and where the chances to find a "real" American are very low.

What we dislike is Americans' disinterest and lack of knowledge about the environment. They consume food and throw garbage away without thinking what happens to the environment. That makes us a bit angry.

The American tipping system has also irritated us for a long time. In Europe, we are used to giving tips based on how satisfied we are with the service. In America, we must give everyone tips, even to those who give terrible service.

Americans like to be independent. Our friends and coworkers in America are used to, and also enjoy, taking care of themselves. They save money for their kids, pay insurance, and take care of everything. It's really important to be a "self-made man" in America.

"I've seen Americans who watch three TV shows at the same time—they just constantly switch between the channels."

Nadine, Tunisia

BRINGING DISGRACE UPON THEIR COUNTRY

I THINK THE USA is quickly going backwards in so many ways and I'm seriously concerned about what will happen to the U.S. if it doesn't change its approach to the world. If we look at the ignorance that today's young Americans have toward the rest of the world, I fear strongly for America's future. The young ones are so incompetent when it comes to knowledge of geography, their own language and history, but they willingly and eagerly take anyone down with racist, incompetent, wrongly-spelled comments on any social media platform. They spread their bullshit, hateful comments without thinking about the person on the receiving end. It seems like tolerance is turned to rage in the USA, and the racism there is now out of proportion—it's appalling. I don't see a bright future for a country with so many incompetent young people who bring disgrace upon their country. In the future, the USA will be an unattractive, remote place for the rest of the world if something dramatic doesn't change soon. I think countries in Asia, like Japan, South Korea and China, are more attractive to people than America in the areas of business, tourism, exports, technology and entertainment. The Asian countries also understand and respect other cultures and traditions. Furthermore, I am sure that many Americans themselves are feeling shame and contempt on behalf of these kids, so now is the time to act. I am tired of seeing the country I once loved collapsing.

Charlotte, Australia

THE AMERICA I KNEW

THE AMERICA I knew was a wonderful place, where people from all over the world visited to find security, peace and freedom. The America I knew was a place for outsiders in the world who dared to be different, where the Jew, the Muslim and the Christian sat together to have a cup of coffee and a talk. The America I knew would accept anyone from anywhere as long as you followed the simplest rules of society—don't bother other people. The America I knew could have any faith or skin color, and could dress the way they wanted to. The Americans I knew would accept each every person exactly as they were. The America I knew has changed.

I still believe that America is better than many other places in the world when it comes to religious freedom, but after 9/11 I have seen a continuous increase of blind religious hate. I was at the tragic place known as Ground Zero right after 9/11 and I paid my respects. I think any blind terror like that, or any kind of terror attack at all is objectionable. 99.999… percent of the people in the world detest terror. But that specific tragic event on 9/11 doesn't justify today's daily racism on the Internet, at schools or in any other area. It's, unfortunately, very easy to witness that racism still exists in America today and the people are blind and cruel. As long as you don't look like a white native European-American, you will likely get racist comments made about you. One example is when Indian-American Nina Davuluri won the 2014 Miss America Pageant. Minutes after, Twitter exploded with racially stupid comments like, "Nice slap in the face to the people of 9/11, how pathetic," "Congratulations to AL.Qaeda" (It is spelled Al-Qaida, by the way) and "Miss America is a terrorist." Another example of loads of racist comments aimed at "terrorists" was when the South Korean band Girls Generation won "Best Video of the Year" for the YouTube Awards in New York City in 2013. How people can even compare South Korean pop artists and an Indian-American Miss America contest winner with a terror organization is impossible for me to understand. It really seems like the young Americans today, first of all, have a lack of competence to understand what's going on in the real world. But worst of all, an aggression toward everything that seems to be different to what they are used to—that aggression has to be dealt with right now. It can't increase.

Blind racial values like that make me annoyed, and I'm sure that if the victims of 9/11 could see these statements on the Internet, they would be very embarrassed and disappointed on behalf of America. Americans must change, too; before 9/11 they were human and tolerant. Americans can't let the new youth take over a nation with so much underlying hate in it.

René Zografos

"Even the old are young-at-heart in America."

Valentina, Croatia

"When an American is meeting a person for the first time, it's like that American has known the stranger his whole life. It's like, 'Hey best buddy!'"

Daniel, Netherland

DEAR BROTHER

Mark Manson left the U.S. in 2009 to live in South America. He traveled around Latin America, Europe and Asia for a few years and eventually decided to just never go back. He has visited over forty countries, and he has had the time to reflect over his former home country.

THE UNITED STATES is my alcoholic brother. And although I will always love him, I don't want to be near him at the moment.

I know that's harsh, but I really feel my home country is not in a good place these days. That's not a socio-economic statement, but rather, a cultural one. The point is we don't really get perspective on what's close to us until we spend time away from it. Just like you didn't realize the weird quirks and nuances of your family until you left and spent time with others, the same is true for country and culture. You often don't see what's messed up about your country and culture until you step outside of it.

And so, even though this opinion is going to come across as fairly scathing, I want the American to know: some of the stuff we do, some of the stuff that we always assumed was normal, is kind of screwed up. And that's OK, because that's true with every culture. It's just easier to spot in others, so we don't always notice it in ourselves.

So, as you read this, know that I'm saying everything with tough love—the same tough love with which I'd sit down and lecture an alcoholic family member. It doesn't mean I don't love you. It doesn't mean there aren't some awesome things about you! And it doesn't mean I'm some saint either, because God knows I'm pretty screwed up—I'm American, after all. There are just a few things you need to hear. And as a friend, I'm going to tell them to you.

There's no way to say this without it coming off as offensive, but a lot of the ways Americans interact comes off as inauthentic or fake to other people. I don't think Americans realize this. I think we've always lived with it, so we think it's normal. I think it happens because our culture is so status-obsessed, so everything has to be "the best thing ever," or "you'll never believe this," even when it's quite mundane. Social status and popularity are idolized a lot more in American culture, so I think that's where you get a lot of the fake niceness. Speaking personally, one of the greatest benefits to living my life outside of the U.S. is that I feel my communication and relationships are far more real and honest these days. I don't think I would have gotten that if I hadn't left.

Because life in the U.S. is so insulated from the outside world, people from the U.S. tend to have delusional higher beliefs about themselves. I don't think this is due to lack of self-esteem, but rather it is due to just ignorance.

Mark Manson

I think the U.S. is extremely fixated on wealth, but more specifically, social status and "having made it". It's the pernicious side effects of the so-called "American Dream". Anybody can be whatever they want, but because of that, if you fail, it means you're a loser, and lazy and stupid, and you suck. A really unique, and not always healthy, culture develops from that, I think. The entire U.S. brand is based on big dreams: Hollywood, NYC, entrepreneurship, and so on. It's the place where supposedly anybody who is smart enough and works hard enough can make it. So that attracts the best and the brightest in the world, and those who think they are the best and brightest in the world, but are not. I think the U.S. is a great option if you are a brilliant tech whiz with a start-up idea or if you are good with numbers and stats and want to make a boatload of money. If you are neither of those things, then you're probably better off elsewhere. The dirty little secret of the US is that the majority of the population doesn't live very well, while the culture reinforces this delusional idea that they are somehow winners.

Most Americans know that the outside world is not that dangerous. The murder rate in a number of U.S. cities is higher than many places in the third-world. I tell every young American I speak with to travel. You don't have to live anywhere, but at least get out and see other parts of the world—most of them will surprise you. Americans, for being the so-called leaders of the world, are surprisingly insulated and ignorant about the rest of the world. And the truth is that the U.S. is ceding its power and influence to other countries and cultures and will continue to do so into the next generation. The idea that the American way of life is superior and best in the world is a vestige of the Cold War. Things have changed now. Things are pretty good in other places, and one should at least be aware of that and see it.

The only thing I miss in America is my family and friends, but there are a lot of things I don't miss about America, and a number of things that prevent me from ever wanting to move back to the U.S., like the horrible, horrible food. Also, I find the people to be, generally, loud and desperate for attention. Other things I despise about America include the lack of education in the majority of the population, and needing a car to get everywhere. My clear advice to Americans is that they must get over themselves, work a little less, get healthy, and treat poor people with a little bit more dignity and respect.

A lot is said about the world loving or hating the U.S. I honestly think most people don't really care. They like our movies and our TV shows and they don't really care about most of the other stuff. More educated people have stronger opinions about our politics (specifically, how embarrassing they usually are) and most of them think we're pretty militant and violent as a culture, which, I guess, is kind of true.

The U.S. needs to address its inequality issues. The current system is simply not sustainable. Unfortunately, I think this is unlikely to happen until it's too late. The U.S. is going to lose its preeminence in the world during our lifetime. Hopefully, once it's no longer debatable that America is not in first place all the time, the

country will be forced to look inward and take accountability for its problems.

Few people are impressed by Americans. Unless you're speaking with a real estate agent or a prostitute, chances are they're not going to be excited that you're American. It's not some badge of honor we get to parade around. Yes, we had Steve Jobs and Thomas Edison, but unless you actually *are* Steve Jobs or Thomas Edison, then most people around the world are simply not going to care. There are exceptions, of course, and those exceptions are called English and Australian people. As Americans, we're brought up our entire lives being taught that we're the best, we did everything first and that the rest of the world follows our lead. Not only is this not true, but people get irritated when you bring this attitude with you to their country.

Despite the occasional eye-rolling, and complete inability to understand why anyone would vote for George W. Bush, people from other countries don't hate us, either. In fact—and I know this is a really sobering realization for us—most people in the world don't really think about us or care about us. I know that sounds absurd, especially with CNN and Fox News showing the same twenty angry Arab men on repeat for ten years straight. But unless we're invading someone's country, or threatening to invade someone's country (which is likely), then there's a 99.99 percent chance they don't care about us. Just like we rarely think about the people in Bolivia or Mongolia, most people don't think about us much. They have jobs, kids, house payments—you know, those things called lives to worry about, kind of like us.

Americans tend to assume that the rest of the world either loves us or hates us. The fact is, most people feel neither. Most people don't think much about us. Remember that immature girl in high school, who every little thing that happened to her meant that someone either hated her or was obsessed with her? She was the girl who thought every teacher who ever gave her a bad grade was being totally unfair and everything good that happened to her was because of how amazing she was? Yeah, we're that immature high-school girl.

For all of our talk about being global leaders and how everyone follows us, we don't seem to know much about our supposed "followers." They often have completely different takes on history than we do. We did not invent democracy. We didn't even invent modern democracy. There were parliamentary systems in England and other parts of Europe over a hundred years before we created government. In a recent survey, 63 percent could not find Iraq on a map (despite being at war with them), and 54 percent did not know Sudan was a country in Africa. Yet, somehow we're positive that everyone else looks up to us.

Latin, and some European, cultures describe us as "cold" and "passionless" and for good reason. In our social lives, we don't say what we mean and we don't mean what we say. In our culture, appreciation and affection are implied rather than spoken outright. Two guy friends call each other names to reinforce their friendship, meanwhile men and women tease and make fun of each other to imply interest. Feelings are almost never shared openly and freely. Consumer culture has cheapened our language of gratitude. Something like, "It's so good to see you" is empty now because it's expected and heard from everybody.

In dating, when I find a woman attractive, I almost always walk right up to her and tell her that a) I wanted to meet her, and b) she's beautiful. In America, women usually get incredibly nervous and confused when I do this. They'll make jokes to defuse the situation or sometimes ask me if I'm part of a TV show or playing a prank. Even when they're interested and go on dates with me, they get a bit disoriented when I'm so blunt with my interest. Whereas, in almost every other culture, approaching women this way is met with a confident smile and a "Thank you."

As John Steinbeck famously said, the problem with poor Americans is that, "They don't believe they're poor, but rather temporarily embarrassed millionaires." It's this culture of self-delusion that allows America to continue to innovate and churn out new industry more than anyone else in the world. But this shared delusion also, unfortunately, keeps perpetuating large social inequalities and the quality of life for the average citizen is lower than most other developed countries. It's the price we pay to maintain our growth and economic dominance.

In 2010, I got into a taxi in Bangkok to take me to a new six-story cineplex. It was accessible by metro, but I chose a taxi instead. On the seat in front of me was a sign with a Wi-Fi password. Wait, what? I asked the driver if he had Wi-Fi in his taxi. He flashed a huge smile. The squat Thai man, with his Pidgin English, explained that he had installed it himself. He then turned on his new sound system and disco lights. His taxi instantly became a cheesy nightclub on wheels... with free Wi-Fi.

If there's one constant in my travels over the past three years, it has been that almost every place I've visited, especially in Asia and South America, is much nicer and safer than I expected it to be. Singapore is pristine. Hong Kong makes Manhattan look like a suburb. My neighborhood in Colombia is nicer than the one where I lived in Boston.

As Americans, we have this naïve assumption that people all over the world are struggling and way behind us. They're not. Sweden and South Korea have more advanced, high-speed Internet networks. Japan has the most advanced trains and transportation systems. Norwegians make more money. The biggest and most advanced plane in the world is flown out of Singapore. The tallest buildings in the world are now in Dubai and Shanghai. Meanwhile, the U.S. has the highest incarceration rate in the world.

Not only are we emotionally insecure as a culture, but I've also come to realize how paranoid we are about our physical security. You don't have to watch Fox News or CNN for more than ten minutes to hear about how our drinking water is going to kill us, our neighbor is going to rape our children and some terrorist in Yemen is coming for us. There's a reason we have more guns than people. In the U.S., security trumps everything, even liberty. We're paranoid.

I've probably been to ten countries now that friends and family back home told me explicitly not to go to because someone was going to kill me, kidnap me, stab me, rob me, rape me, sell me into sex trade, give me HIV or whatever else. None of that has happened. I've never been robbed, and I've walked through some of the shittiest parts of Asia, Latin America and Eastern Europe.

In fact, the experience has been the opposite. In countries like Russia, Colombia or Guatemala, people were so honest and open with me it actually scared me. Some stranger in a bar would invite me to his house for a barbecue with his family, a random person on the street would offer to show me around and give me directions to a store I was trying to find. My American instincts were always like, "Wait, this guy is going to try to rob me or kill me?" but they never did. They were just insanely friendly.

I've noticed that the way we Americans communicate is usually designed to create a lot of attention and hype. Again, I think this is a product of our consumer culture: the belief that something isn't worthwhile or important unless it's perceived to be the best ever.

This is why Americans have a peculiar habit of thinking everything is "totally awesome" and even the most mundane activities were "the best thing ever". It's the unconscious drive we share for importance and significance, this unmentioned belief, socially beaten into us since birth that if we're not the best at something, then we don't matter.

We're status-obsessed. Our culture is built around achievement, production and being exceptional. Therefore, comparing ourselves and attempting to out-do one another has infiltrated our social relationships as well. Who can slam the most beers first? Who can get reservations at the best restaurant? Who knows the promoter to the club? Who dated a girl on the cheerleading squad? Socializing becomes objectified and turned into a competition. And if you're not winning, the implication is that you are not important and no one will like you.

Unless you have cancer or something equally dire, the health care system in the U.S. sucks. The World Health Organization rates the U.S. thirty-seventh in the world for health care, despite the fact that we spend the most per capita by a large margin. The hospitals are nicer in Asia, with European-educated doctors and nurses, and cost one-tenth as much. Something as routine as a vaccination costs several hundred dollars in the U.S. and less than ten dollars in Colombia. And before you make fun of Colombian hospitals, Colombia is twenty-eighth in the world on that W.H.O. list, nine spots higher than us.

My health insurance costs the past year? Sixty-five dollars per month. Why? Because I live outside of the U.S. An American guy I met living in Buenos Aires got knee surgery for free that would have cost $10,000 in the U.S. But this isn't really getting into the real problems of our health. Our food is killing us. I'm not going to go crazy with the details, but we eat chemically-laced crap because it's cheaper and tastes better—profit, profit. Our portion sizes are absurd—more profit. And we're by far the most prescribed nation in the world and our drugs cost five-to-ten times more than they do in other countries, even Canada.

In terms of life expectancy, despite being the richest country in the world, we come in a paltry thirty-eighth. Right behind Cuba, Malta and the United Arab Emirates, and slightly ahead of Slovenia, Kuwait and Uruguay. Enjoy your Big Mac.

The United States is a country built on the exaltation of economic growth and personal ingenuity. Small businesses and constant growth are celebrated and supported above all else—above affordable health care, above respectable education, above everything. Americans believe it's your responsibility to take care of yourself and make something of yourself, not the state's, not your community's, not even your friend's or family's in some instances.

Comfort sells easier than happiness. Comfort is easy—it requires no effort and no work. Happiness takes effort. It requires being proactive, confronting fears, facing difficult situations and having unpleasant conversations.

Comfort equals sales. We've been sold comfort for generations and for generations we've bought bigger houses (separated farther and farther out into the suburbs), bigger TVs, more movies and more take-out food. The American public is becoming docile and complacent. We're obese and entitled. When we travel, we look for giant hotels that will insulate us and pamper us rather than for legitimate cultural experiences that may challenge our perspectives or help us grow as individuals. Depression and anxiety disorders are soaring within the U.S. Our inability to confront anything unpleasant around us has not only created a national sense of entitlement, but it's disconnected us from what actually drives happiness: relationships, unique experiences, feeling self-validated and achieving personal goals. It's easier to watch a NASCAR race on television and tweet about it than to actually get out and try something new with a friend. Unfortunately, a by-product of our massive commercial success is that we're able to avoid the necessary emotional struggles of life in lieu of easy, superficial pleasures.

Throughout history, every dominant civilization eventually collapsed because it became too successful. Whatever made the civilization powerful and unique grows out of proportion and consumes its society. I think this is true for American society. We're complacent, entitled and unhealthy. My generation is the first generation of Americans who will be worse off than their parents, economically, physically and emotionally. And this is not due to a lack of resources, to a lack of education or to a lack of ingenuity—it's corruption and complacency. The corruption stems from the massive industries that control our government's policies, and the fat complacency is from the people who sit around and let it happen.

There are things I love about my country. I don't hate the U.S. and I still return to it a few times a year. But I think the greatest flaw of American culture is our blind self-absorption. In the past, this trait only hurt other countries. But now, we're starting to hurt ourselves. So this is my lecture to my alcoholic brother—my own flavor of arrogance and self-absorption, even if slightly more informed—in hopes he'll give up his wayward ways. I imagine it'll fall on deaf ears, but it's the most I can do for now. Now if you'll excuse me, I have some funny cat pictures to look at.

Mark Manson, American ex-patriot, www.markmanson.net

THREE RANDOM PEOPLE FROM GERMANY

"America has all these cool gadgets that you don't know that you need until you try them, but that are fun to have. For example, I have just tried out an American electric adjustable bed—it's so fantastic, my boyfriend also loves it."

Kathrin, Germany

"Cheerleaders must be the greatest gift to the American society."

Felix, Germany

"Foreigners think that American patriotism is too fanatic, with the president's picture and the American flag on the wall. But as long as they don't go extreme—I mean it's healthy that people are proud of their nation. But everyone must be aware that it is a thin line, because other people may think you are extreme even if you're not."

Alfred, Germany

WORDS OF WISDOM

1. *"The American lives even more for his goals, for the future, than the European. Life for him is always becoming, never being."*

   Albert Einstein, German physicist

2. *"I love the United States, but I see here everything is measured by success, by how much money it makes, not the satisfaction to the individual."*

   John Fellows Akers, businessman and president of IBM

3. *"We must stop talking about the American dream and start listening to the dreams of Americans."*

   Reubin Askew, Governor

4. *"What the people want is very simple—they want an America as good as its promise."*

   Barbara Charline Jordan, American politician

5. *"If American men are obsessed with money, American women are obsessed with weight. The men talk of gain, the women talk of loss, and I do not know which talk is the more boring."*

   Marya Mannes, American writer

6. *"The American ideal is youth, handsome, empty youth."*

> Henry Miller, American writer

7. *"The American, by nature, is optimistic. He is experimental, an inventor and a builder who builds best when called upon to build greatly."*

> John F. Kennedy, former U.S. President

8. *"This American system of ours—call it Americanism, call it capitalism, call it what you like—gives to each and every one of us a great opportunity if we only seize it with both hands and make the most of it."*

> Al Capone, Italian-American gangster

9. *"The American people are a very generous people and will forgive almost any weakness, with the possible exception of stupidity."*

Will Rogers, American cowboy, comedian, humorist, social commentator, vaudeville performer and actor

10. *"Whoever wants to know the heart and mind of America had better learn baseball."*

Jacques Martin Barzun, French-born, American historian

11. *"The American mind, unlike the English, is not formed by books, but, as Carl Sandburg once said to me, by newspapers and the Bible."*

Van Wyck Brooks, American literary critic, biographer and historian

12. *"I think there are only three things America will be known for 2,000 years from now when they study this civilization: the Constitution, jazz music and baseball."*

Gerald Early, American Essayist

ON A REMOTE ISLAND IN THE INDIAN OCEAN

Koh Kho Khao is a distant island in the Indian Ocean with a very low population. Luckily, I met these two guys there.

AMERICANS ALWAYS BUY three or four suits and shirts when they visit me. They are always polite and nice. They know what good quality is, and appreciate what we can offer. Russians and Chinese are the worst customers I get. They don't know anything about style, quality and clothes like Americans do. I really don't know why they bother to come in and visit me at all because they never buy anything. The Russians and the Chinese are awful and are destroying this island. I wish every customer in the world were exactly like Americans.

Marco, tailor at Koh Kho Khao Island and also in Bangkok

Americans seem to be cool people, but something is missing over there, and that is the care for their family. In Thailand, the family, and especially the ladies, comes first. We always protect our family, and we learn from what life gives us. In America, the care for the family is, unfortunately, not their first priority.

For me, the American girls are unserious. They like to play a lot before anything gets serious, and the girls are very focused on money. Americans always struggle to get a lot of money, like Donald Trump, but are they happier than us? It doesn't seem so. Mr. Trump, by the way, seems to be a smart guy, but he is, along with other Americans in the USA, what we call in Thailand very "sticky," otherwise known as too glossy and smooth to be called a real man.

When Americans drink too much, they turn bad, and shout a lot—no one on earth likes that, so it's a mystery to me why they keep on doing that.

Another thing we don't like is that Americans have appointed themselves as a big godfather to the world—they bring their power and military forces to any country they find interesting, end of discussion.

There is only one thing I really love about America, and that is Mr. Harley Davidson. My dream is to travel around America on my Harley, listening to country music and visiting Native Indian villages. I would also like to visit Daytona Beach, Florida, during bike week.

What do I think about American food? "…PUUH!"

Kiam, Hapla Beach, Koh Kho Khao, Thailand

"Americans grow stronger as the problems get bigger."

Helmut, Germany

"America is a young country, but the people are very old-thinking."

My Ling, China

FIVE IN FLORENCE, ITALY

1) *"I love American women. Actually, when I come to think of it, I love all women, but American women most."*

   Luca, Italia

2) *"Americans only flirt with people when they have something to gain."*

   Alessa, Italy

3) *"The Americans girls, they have this funny, big hairstyle—like we had in the eighties."*

   Maurizio, Italy

4) *"How come American fishing boats look like huge containers? They may be functional, but they are not stylish."*

   Niko, Italy

5) *"I wonder: Have all Americans fake white teeth?"*

   Massimo, Italy

AT THE DENTIST'S OFFICE

"THE AMERICANS WHO come to us always want a big, white smile. Even though many of them have a really bad starting point, with really bad teeth, they want their teeth to be so bright, white and shiny, like a newly-painted white wall. But I don't think they look that good when they do that. Americans always end up with a "Mickey Mouse" smile that looks a bit unnatural. Europeans never want teeth as white as the Americans want them.

Most of the Americans come to do huge dental surgery—like doing twenty crowns or something like that. We always say that Americans need an "ear-to-ear job" —that they need to fix all the teeth from one ear to the other. But they are always so satisfied when the job is done, because they always end up with a big white, shiny, but yet unnatural Hollywood smile.

> Zohán, Budapest, Hungary, works at a dental clinic

"There are so many Americans with gold teeth in their mouths. All these gold fillings mean that the American graveyards soon will be the new Klondike."

> Adrian, Germany

"It's not polite to look down on strangers of other nationalities. Americans do that consistently; they consider everyone else in the world to be of less worth than themselves."

Takaho, Japan

"Most people I know are spoiled and born with a silver spoon in their mouth. Many successful Americans have shown that if you have talent and work hard enough, there is no need to be born with that silver spoon. Americans know, and have proven, that anyone can make it on their own."

Richard, New Zealand

SUMMARY

ON SEPTEMBER 6, 2013, world leaders met at the G20 meeting in St. Petersburg, Russia. At the end of the convention, the President of the United States of America held a press conference and talked about a possible reaction from the United Nations concerning the war crimes in Syria using gas and killing 1,400 people, 400 of them innocent small children. With pride and integrity, he explained to our world leaders why they all should react. He mentioned war crimes, use of chemical weapons and killing innocent children, and that the world must say no to cowardly actions such as this, no matter what regime is in power. Many of the world leaders, from nations who are allied with the USA, were dead silent, with no support to the U.S. President. He was speaking to deaf ears. I can't imagine how it must have felt to be the only leader on the whole earth who wanted to take action against such cowardly actions; he sincerely wanted justice and to protect the children in Syria from possible further attacks from chemical weapons. That says a lot about the politicians in the world, including my home country's politicians, who are more focused on secure, good solutions for their own personal interests rather than willing to stand up for what's right and to make a difference in the world. But it also says a lot about the USA and their overall focus on justice and freedom for all the people in the world, and not only for Americans. Even though this book, for the most part, is not about politics, I had to mention this, because the American President illustrated how alone America is sometimes when it comes to protecting human rights and standing up for fairness and liberty. What I have learned about Americans while writing this book is that it's not only the American leaders who have a sense of justice, but, that the American people have true intentions to carry out integrity and justice, too. Believe it or not, that is not a matter of course in many other countries on this globe. To practice freedom, to speak freely and to protect the weakest are principles that are implanted in the whole American nation, from head to toe, even though there are huge class inequalities found in American culture. Therefore, it is really sad to see so many paralyzed leaders of countries who, unfortunately, have no visions to make this planet a better place for all its citizens. Leaders who have sky-scraping power in the world still sit there handicapped and passive in their own wealth. Sometimes I wonder where the empathy in the world has gone. But nobody is perfect, and the USA is no exception. This planet doesn't only need more peace and justice, it also needs harmony. It's also about pollution, toxic waste and sharing from the same world food basket where it's fair to say that Americans had more than one hand into it, even if it's not the case for some Americans who are now living below the poverty line. It's about extreme consumption, but also what the Americans are consuming—Americans are still champions when it comes to devouring. In many conversations, with both Americans and with foreigners, they seem to agree that extreme consumption began early when the immigrants started to build a life to achieve more wealth and freedom in America. It's essentially not problematic to aim for richness—it's how you manage your wealth that can be a problem. For Americans, the American dream and wealth is often synonymous with having a lot of things: several arbitrarily big houses, many big-engine cars and as much food as they can get their hands on. But, to be wealthy can also mean freedom for the individual, the ability to choose your profession, the ability to unwind more, to make a difference to other people, and in some ways many Americans also care for others. When I ask people what's typical for an American, the answer is often charity, fundraising and donations. People in the USA like to give and to help others out, even more so nowadays. It's not hip anymore to sit alone in the back of a big limousine, counting dollars. It's not what a modern American would do. Modern Americans are focused on doing something meaningful and helping others out is the right thing to do for the new and trendier American who has achieved the American dream. Bill and Melinda Gates, for example, have more money than they can spend, but their life wouldn't mean a great deal if they kept their money in the bank and didn't share it with people who needed it. Gates' vaccination program has already saved hundreds of thousands of children's lives. That's an example, among many, of how to manage wealth. After Hurricane Katrina hit the Gulf Coast, and other catastrophes in the USA, we witness how the average American works and helps out others when their neighbors' worlds seem to fall apart. That is how it should be like all over the world, and that is something that should be admirable to the rest of the world.

IS THE AMERICAN DREAM STILL REACHABLE?

YES IT IS, but sorrowfully it doesn't seem to happen as often as before, and that's a challenge for the new America. But we also have to ask ourselves a question: What does the American dream mean to you? Is it necessarily more money, which also includes more hours at the office or at the factory? The dream can also mean more time for friends, connecting to deeper feelings or just a wish to be happier. I know so many people who barely have food on the table, but still are quite happy and content.

It's vital for people to know that anything is still possible if they're doing great things and work hard enough. That vision must never fade out in America because it's something that really is central in the Americans' foundation and spirit. An essential goal for many is to hope for better days—to "make it" and to finally achieve what they aimed for so they can secure their family's future. But nowadays, everybody knows that it's much harder to find fame and fortune. If the American dream dies out, so will the American economy because the future for Americans would then be very uncertain. It would be crucial for America to have passive workers without any ambitions or hopes—a situation we find in some European and African countries where nobody really believes in the future, and with good reason. But let us just look the fact in the eye that the American dream will never die out! The American dream, as we have seen it till now, may have changed—it's no longer about having the most money in your bank account, now it means fairness to all people and to actually have fewer and smaller things—the best things in life are actually free. Americans will always be dreamers, and I mean that in a very positive way because dreamers are the hard workers, dreamers are the innovators of the world and dreamers will always reach out for something better and bigger, and work their asses off till it's done. So, for an American, the American dream is still very much alive, but it can be harder to obtain if it's only material goals you are aiming for, however, remember this: Americans often, somehow, seem to find ways to accomplish their economic goals, as well.

HANDICRAFTS AND THE WORKFORCE

P EOPLE IN THE world are missing American-quality products. Many old American cars still have legendary status in
Europe. To own an old Thunderbird or a Mustang is still
the ultimate joy for many car owners there. Other things, like
American refrigerators, furniture and electronics, were pure quality
to us. So what happened? Since the 1980s we haven't seen many
new American cars in Europe. We now see more old American
cars on the road than new ones. I have never seen an American-
made refrigerator in Norway, but we have lookalikes made in other
countries.

America was known for building top-quality products for
the American market, but the world has become smaller and the
competition is now fiercer. That means that we can get supplies
from all over the world at a very low cost, and that also means that
America must compete with labor skills throughout the world.
Therefore, Americans must also deal with international prices, not
only for export purposes, but also for import use. I don't think
Americans can work more hours than they already do to make the
prices drop lower; Americans are already the hardest working people in the world. Americans can never compete with Asian workers
when it comes to labor costs, and they shouldn't do that anyway.
Americans should do what they do best: make quality products,
continue manufacturing and being innovative. People worldwide

want quality products encased in great packaging. So, if Americans can gain the status they had before of making the best products in the world, products that look and feel good, then people will embrace American goods. One example and exception is Apple. (I'm in a small café in Oslo, Norway right now, and I can see five Apple MacBooks and three Apple iPhones from where I am sitting. No other brands are displayed.) Apple has innovated quality products for years, and even though Apple products may be twenty times more expensive than a competing product, people still buy them more than other products. So the question we must ask is: Why are we buying their stuff? We buy Apple because they are great products and they work well, but also because they look outstanding and they are a kind of fashion statement for customers. Kitchen Aid and Tesla electric cars are other examples that have had success outside of America. They share a common trait: above-average quality. This quality focus is exactly the right direction for America to go. People in the world sincerely miss American-quality products. Make cool cars again, produce organic, healthy food that the world customers want now, do your own manufacturing and make sure that you make pure, high-quality products—don't take shortcuts. Let "Made in America" be the highest quality statement in the world. If you do, you will find customers that are ready to pay for it. This is the only way to go, not only for survival, but also to again become an important and attractive part of a global perspective. This will also bring the middle class back up to decent salaries, and, secondarily, give them better rights and negotiating opportunities. No country will stay healthy without a strong middle class that spends money. That is essential for all of America. Look what made America so great in the past and you will find the answers to be manufacturing, quality and innovation; these keywords seem to be essential for any country that has healthy economic development for all of their citizens and not only for a few billionaires. Such positive actions will also bring about good synergy effects; it will bring back dignity and future hope, but also give more freedom for workers who can choose their employer and follow the career they desire.

Americans who want their goods out in the world must also learn to adjust their products for each and every country because they have all different needs. You can't, for example, sell a lot of Ford Explorers in many places in Asia because the streets are too small and the traffic is too congested. A big car like that is also too expensive for low- and middle-class economies in Asia. In India, where they have over one billion citizens, they sell more scooters and motorcycles than cars, so in such places you have to sell two-wheelers or very small, cheap cars. The possibilities are endless in places like that; the products just need adjustment and cultural understanding. Americans must learn and respect other countries' cultures; this alone will make it a lot easier to recognize their needs and to do business with them. We must also keep in mind that the majority of people in the world want to keep our environment in a good condition and, therefore, we will, and we must, change to smaller, more efficient vehicles and other environmentally-friendly products. That is a challenge all companies must take on, and this challenge will separate the losers from the winners in the future.

TIME OFF

I WAS ACTUALLY A bit surprised when I found out that American workers have so little time off from work. I have always thought that Japan, or maybe China, was the leader when it comes to time spent at work, but American workers surpassed them long ago. Something is wrong when a person must have two or three jobs to pay their bills and to put food on the table. But I also now understand that the work ethic is different and stronger in the U.S. than in many other countries, and that many Americans live for, but also enjoy, their jobs. Still, it should be possible to live on one salary, and I believe that you get better workers if you pay them well and let them have some time off once in a while. But business owners will never give away vacations for free. The mandate must come from the government to give all Americans statutory weeks of holidays. In my country, we have five weeks every year for every worker, and six weeks for people over the age of sixty. We also have days off at Christmas and Easter. So why can't a country like America afford to have more time off? To start gradually with two consecutive weeks of time off for all the Americans workers is, to me, a good idea. It will be paid back with a motivated, loyal, hardworking staff, and will probably also help the surgery and heart attack statistics at American hospitals. In other words, it can be a win-win situation; the business owner gets healthier and more motivated employees, while the U.S. government gets healthier citizens that cost less in social spending.

TV PROBLEMS

EVERY PROFESSIONAL SHRINK in the world would say that human contact is necessary for the human race. Nevertheless, there seems to be less contact between human beings in the USA now than ever before. There is also a tendency for loneliness in other places in the world, but people seem to agree that Americans are in the real danger zone now—there are too many people on the outskirts of daily social interactions, and young people, in particular, are ostracized from socialization and they grow very lonely. Individuals must have human contact, but if they are not getting it, they will not stay healthy in the long run. In fact, in older civilizations, they punished people by making them lonely forever when they had done something bad—no one was allowed to speak to them at all, and such punishment was considered the worst sentence a human being could get. That tells us that in social development nowadays, when people spend extensive amounts of time alone without choosing it for themselves, it is very unhealthy. We can blame it on computer games, social media sites like Facebook, wealth and also on the time pressures many of us experience. Yes, it's easier and faster to Skype a friend rather than visit them physically, but it's likely healthier to talk to your friend in real life, to shake hands, spend time together outside and maybe give them a hug. Many of us also have the idea that we don't need to spend time with other people in our daily lives, but deep down inside we should all admit that it is wrong to be all alone for too long a time; it's not good for our mental health or our surroundings. Even though we are all different and have diverse needs, it is essential for us to have human contact. Some people need more, some less, but don't fool yourself and let your life pass by without socializing with other people. Let's now focus on a possible solution: If Americans could manufacture more products, this would automatically involve many of the people who are left unemployed, lonely and on the outskirts of society today. Give people jobs, but also attractive places to meet. Give people hope for the future. Involve everyone in outdoor activities—I mean everyone—people with disabilities, people with psychological problems, everyone. It's been proven many times that being with other people improves mental health.

At the same time, it's important to exclude people who put us down, people who don't give us the right energy. People around the world believe that Americans must learn to bring new people into their lives, people who can give them more joy and strength. There's no point in keeping people in our lives that do not give us any energy, bolster us up or show affection toward us. There are certainly so many wonderful people out there in the world to like, if you just get out that door and try to meet them.

That Americans are jammed in front of their TVs and computers is nothing new to the world audience, and that is something that many have pointed out in my interviews. I think we all can agree that sitting in front of different screens is stealing too much time from our lives. Europeans now have the same problems that Americans have, but people in Europe think that there's one thing that really separates them from the Americans—that they like to have a TV-break and they like to be active and spend time outdoors with others. When we have had our ample time in front of the TV screen, we get restless and must have a breather. During our break, we like to go outdoors, and many of us like to spend time enjoying nature, while some like to socialize and others like to do something physical. Americans don't seem to have the gene that says enough is enough.

Many foreigners have the assumption that Americans can spend their whole life inside their own den, as long as they have good entertainment on a TV screen. They say that many Americans like to have a virtual escape rather than facing the real world. And people are actually quite overwhelmed of the stamina that Americans have when it comes to TV watching; they're amazed that Americans rarely get tired of TV entertainment, and that if they do, they just switch between different activities inside their homes, from watching TV, to surfing on the Internet, to playing videogames. To do something outside that makes them sweat seems to not be an option for them. That kind of misuse of American home entertainment can make people mentally unbalanced, lonely and unhappy. This fact is confirmed by more and more experts all over the world, and nowadays, there are clinics for TV, smart phone and videogame abuse in America. In other countries, like China, we can find similar clinics.

DID YOU KNOW?

Playstation 4, which was released in November, 2013, sold over one million units in North America during the first twenty-four hours it was on sale. In comparison, Playstation 3 sold 197,000 items during the entire first month of sales in 2006.

To witness others folks' happy lives on TV, while their own life and future plans are fading to zero, seems to be hard to deal with for many Americans who otherwise are born with future ambitions and expectations.

The various opinions stated in this book are, of course, not universally true for the entire American population; there are always exceptions, and no two Americans are identical. But still, people believe that many Americans are chained to different TV screens most of their lives, and this is the reason why we find so many lonely, unhappy and disturbed people in the country.

To be more social and to be outside and more in tune with nature seems to be the right way to go for the mental health of America. That challenge acquires a great amount of seriousness for all future Americans, from the single parent to the top leaders.

HOW WE WANT OUR AMERICANS TO BE

SOME THINGS ARE common for all nations in the world: we don't like fake people who try to appear different than they are, we like open, sincere folks, and there is a clear line between "being different" and "acting different." Many people like to discover the unique qualities and personalities of others, how strangers' personalities can suddenly shine on people they randomly meet. We also like people who can make mistakes—individuals who are not flawless. It is part of human nature to make mistakes; to make a blunder or two, once in a while, is actually rather charming to others. To display your talents, but also your flaws, will make people laugh with you, not at you. And to go around and be afraid that someone might not like you the way you are is much too tiresome way to live. There will always be people out there who will not be fond of you, but never use your forces to try to please them or to change yourself to fit their criteria. If they don't accept you as you are, they will probably never accept you at all—especially not if you try to be someone you are not. But luckily, for all of us, there are many people out there that will always like and love us exactly as we are. Our focus should be on them, in addition to ourselves.

Why am I telling you this? Many people I have talked to are saying that a type of "fakeness" and a lack of sincerity exist in the U.S.—that Americans have an inner wish to appear perfect to others, and to show a perfect shell rather than showing their true selves. They think it's more important to let somebody see a happy person instead of being truly happy. But, and actually many Americans

181

will agree, people don't like artificial folks. People like honesty, and most of us don't care if an American lives in a tent or a castle, drives a Porsche or a Vespa, if their suit is from Versace or Gap or if you have a wrinkle or two. People want Americans' uniqueness and genuineness. They want to see you and know you're true; they want your sincere behavior and opinions.

Many also say that plastic surgery, Botox, extreme makeovers and diets are synonymous with Americans. For outsiders, that hysteric behavior, to look as young as possible, is a mystery because, in general, people are very fond of Americans and their non-discrimination to older-looking people. So why do people have to do such makeovers to look extremely young? Is it just difficult for them to accept the process of aging? Americans at the age of seventy and up who are wrinkle-free, full of Botox and have brilliant white teeth, will not earn more respect than any of your fellow citizens who grow old with dignity, and especially not from the young ones. In other words, there are not many benefits of pretending. So why are Americans doing it? Can it be the glamour from Hollywood, or is it all the pressure from society as a whole to appear perfect?

Looking fabulous at work and spreading great Twitter and Instagram images of ourselves is now a part of human behavior all over the world, so that alone can't explain it. So, what is really wrong?

Many people that I have interviewed also say that Americans exaggerate when they talk, and that Americans seem to be high on themselves and gladly share their own sovereignty stories with everyone else as often as they can. People also say that this American superficial, smug behavior is a clear symptom of low self-esteem, but that it is also an indication of modest self-knowledge.

If we summarize this feedback and put it in perspective, I think we will find one conclusion. I have no doubt that the pressure to perform and appear great in the U.S. is greater than many other places that I know of. I have met many Americans that say that they always must be at their best, and by best, they mean best on each and every top level, at all times. They must look good, they must have the best ideas, do great at school, excel in sports, they must work harder than their colleagues and the daily competition never really seems to stop for them!

The Americans also have a tremendous pressure to be successful in each and every period of their lives. It starts very early—even as babies Americans can get rated—and it continues through all levels of schooling and career, and through the very end of their life cycle. In the opinion of many, that kind of community cannot stay healthy for any individual in the long run, and it must be hard to practice a never-ending and very stressful contest every day of your life when there are not, in reality, any clear winners at the finish line. That crazy contest should stop now.

But it can also mean that the USA is at the forefront of a superficial population trend that is increasing rapidly in many parts of the world. Even we Europeans are not on an American level, yet I can still feel some of the same pressure here in Europe; we are probably just some years behind.

I can, of course, advise Americans and everyone else in the world to drop the artificial intervention on their own body. Why pay a lot of money for something that doesn't come out better than before? But also, why try to behave as someone that you're not? Enjoy your wrinkles when they come, eat natural food that keeps you naturally young longer, be humble, embrace your faults, be sad, be happy, be kind, be yourself—at least, that's how people outside of American borders want their Americans to live.

"America is a place where many parents live their dreams through their kids' lives. I think that these parents must start to live their own lives and let their kids find dreams of their own."

Anita, Ghana

"It's a common fact that Americans brag about everything, but it's also a fact that they, most of all, love to brag about themselves."

Miriam, Pakistan

POSITIVE ATTENTION, PLEASE

L
OVE... FEEL THE word. Have you ever tasted real love before? Doesn't it taste great? Doesn't it touch you when you hear that specific word from someone? The word almost melts on my tongue every time I say it. The word gives me a feeling unlike any other word. It can tell me that I'm very special to someone. It's a word we should use when we need to express our greatest affection—a word we only use when the biggest things in life happen to us. But nowadays, the word is, sadly, used too often on random daily subjects. It's 'love this' and 'love that,' 'love, love everywhere.' What happened to 'like'? Or 'enjoy'? Aren't these words used anymore? Can't we say, "I like something" without using huge, exceptional words in every sentence? Many think that Americans are using the highest superlatives for the most daily basic things. Must they do that to be visible in today's community in America? And if it is so, what comes next? What about the day they really need to express themselves to someone? How will Americans then articulate their thoughts and feelings without using cliché-words, like what "love" has become?

We are all screaming for attention, and it seems like many are using major adjectives to get noticed, but people are saying that Americans are undoubtedly ahead on this particular issue. Americans like more attention than people from any other nation, and foreigners really wonder why they do. It's undeniable that the human race wants positive attention, and to live in America during the social media generation just makes it ten times more important to have a lot of attention. Nowadays, everybody can observe you through the web—your teacher, the one you have a crush on, your daughter, your boss, your friends—anyone. It's important for you to be attractive to all of them. When I was in primary school, the most feared subject was writing. Now, writing is a necessity to be a part of the social media world, where most of the youngsters communicate today. Believe it or not, it was actually possible to have a life without writing and photography skills in the earlier days. Nowadays, that is impossible if you don't want to be anonymous to the rest of your world. American youngsters have learned how important it is to be well-liked on social media platforms. Unfortunately, such media is also open for people who have harmful motives, people that do their best to denigrate others. It's easy to sit here and say that posting hurtful comments on the Internet will not have any effect on others, but the reality is that every day, people are having terrible days because of bullies on the web. As a consequence, young people in America will, in the future, continue to take their own lives after reading a bad comment about their self-published picture. That tells us that we must be very cautious when we write our comments because to be perceived as perfect as possible is crucial in America.

This also creates a dilemma on the flip side because there are people who like to be the center of attention and feel the need to be active on every popular social media platform, post well-expressed messages, cool videos and stunning pictures of themselves frequently, just to get attention. On the other hand, their attention-seeking behaviors put them in a vulnerable position because someone may comment on their post in a negative way. And that is not what today's youngsters want in America—they want, and must have, positive attention!

It's not only average people who want this kind of attention in America. We can see how pop stars like Britney Spears and Miley Cyrus take drastic action to get more attention, like performing nearly naked on a stage or in a video. But for them it could also possibly be a way to hide a lack of talent; they must show sides of themselves other than singing to maintain their popularity. But many gifted Americans don't need that kind of extra attention; they are confident about their own work.

Everybody should understand that they are good enough, so bad comments shouldn't affect you, rather you should see them for what they truly are: just uncertainty from the messenger. And remember, we can all get positive attention somehow. Some people are great dancers, some are great engineers, others great craftsmen. All of us have something that can give us positive praise. The problem is when we want positive attention in all areas. We must stop thinking that we must be great at everything. Americans must stop and breathe; focus on what you do best. If you are a great basketball player, focus on that. If you are genius in mathematics, enjoy that wonderful gift you have received. If your goal is to be a good singer or a songwriter, follow that path. And tell others what you're good at, but don't overdo it, because people will then get the impression that you brag about yourself. And as I mentioned earlier, people think Americans are pretty high on themselves already, so to tell others about your skills is quite fine, but to boast out about everything you do is quite unattractive, according to the citizens of the world. That message to the American people has come through pretty clear throughout my interviews.

I also think this issue is a matter of cultural differences. Americans are used to talking about their victories and skills to others, so a fellow American can handle more self-bragging than foreigners. Where I come from, but also in many other countries in the world, if someone says something like, "I am good at something," it is easily perceived as self-serving, and that is negative in countries other than the U.S. In America, saying the same thing will be understood as positive and admirable. If I had to choose between the two, I would actually like to have it more like the American way, but with some elements of moderation; it's actually possible to like something without loving it.

AMERICAN EATING HABITS

AMERICAN NUTRITION IS a chapter of its own. It's everything from unhealthy junk food to extremely unhealthy diets. Let's start with the worst first: junk food. Abroad, Americans have been famous for their burgers and fries for ages, and, in a way, such junk food has become a part of the daily diet in many parts of the world. Sadly, at the same time, we have seen a critical increase of obesity and diseases in the U.S. Now, we also find very chunky people in other parts of the world, like India, where they eat more and more "American-style." It's called Western diseases. In this book, we have already covered some of the problems with Western junk food, and for me, it's impossible to understand why so many Americans can accept all the unnatural food they are getting. Before, when we didn't know better, it was understandable, but not anymore now that we have all this information. I have been in the U.S. many times, and it upsets me every time to see so much easy, cheaply-accessible, terrible food. We can argue forever about what kind of food is best for humans, but if we look at it from an evolutionary perspective, we can all see that natural human food like organic meat, healthy fat, wild fish and vegetables have been the main foodstuff humans have been eating since we came to the earth. The exception is found in these most recent decades when the food industry became all about manipulating food as we know it. It's terrible, unethical and dishonest that

American citizens get pumped with artificial ingredients that give them unbearable pains for a lifetime. It can't be in the interest of a huge company to decide which food the American people get on their dinner table! In general, I don't advocate too much regulation, but when it comes to American nutrition and all the suffering the Americans have had to put up with for so many years, I would like to have very strict rules in this area, and even laws, that stop companies from making food that injures and kills American people every day. It's their right as American citizens to protect themselves, and the thing that really threatens them is disreputable, greedy food producers. It's time for the American people to stand up and say that they don't want to eat food with poison and artificial ingredients in it anymore. Americans must, in my opinion, put up the barricades on this issue because no one else is there to protect them. It's every American's responsibility and duty to keep their family safe and healthy, and it must, of course, be a right for every American to have access to natural healthy food that doesn't kill them. But it really also is the American leaders and, finally, the American President who hold an overall responsibility to make sure that healthy food is available to all the people in the U.S. I understand that there are jobs and political interests to be maintained, but the bottom line is asking what's more important: people's health or making huge, rich companies richer? The American President must also understand that bad fuel creates sick people that don't work as well as they should and that the community costs, because of that, are much higher than they should be. People need to know what kind of food is tampered and manipulated with and what food is clean. This way they can start to choose for themselves if they want non-poisonous food or not. But, we can all do something right now. We can start to eat organic food and cook our own meals; we can go to our local grocery and demand them to provide us with organic food. That will help you and your family right now, but it must really come as an overall, non-negotiable requirement from all Americans that unhealthy food must be forbidden, and that poisonous food is something that they won't eat anymore. Such a demand will make all of America much healthier.

American super diets are also rather well known around the world, and many foreigners are using them. But most foreigners are actually joking about them, especially the extreme diets you have that promise extreme changes in just a few days. It's very odd for many foreigners to see how Americans abuse their body for years with bad food, then suddenly change to an extreme diet a few weeks before the bikini season starts, and then turn back to junk food again right after the end of that season.

Bad eating habits are now creating obesity, serious diseases and enormous pain for many people in the world. In India, where McDonalds now is available in almost every city and also in the small towns, millions of kids have diabetes, cancer, weight problems and life-threatening diseases—problems that were almost absent until a few years ago.

But to be fair, we can't blame America for the food that people around the world eat. They have to take their own responsibility for their junk food abuse and their politics, but in a way, the American lifestyle and the American dream we all hear and see on TV all over the world is quite tempting for the young ones in every country in the world. It unconsciously has created a certain effect on all of us. To be equal with American kids is something to which many of the world's children aspire. But, the result of such desire for the American lifestyle can, in fact, be fatal for them.

AMERICAN EFFICIENCY

HERE, IF I come up with a new proposal for my publisher, or suggest an idea to someone else that they find interesting, it usually takes a long time to bring that idea to life. It doesn't even seem to make a difference if the idea is great or just good, it will take time. To make slow decisions is just how it is here, and it's something we are used to. Some countries are even worse than us, especially in southern parts of Europe where there is a tradition to be ineffective. In America—BOOM—it's done. The whole world enjoys the American "when said, it's done" mentality. I, personally, sometimes can't understand how companies in Europe can survive with proven inertia and dullness on every decision. When such apathy gains breeding ground, it becomes a plague that the whole country must carry.

It seems that Americans are better than most countries, in nearly all areas, when we talk about execution. Even outside of their own country, they are proven to be very effective at getting things accomplished. When people became homeless because of a sudden hurricane in the Philippines in November of 2014, who was first on site to help? Americans. Who was first to help when a Tsunami hit the Indian Ocean in 2004? Americans. While our politicians in Europe are discussing how they should help, the Americans are already there, helping and saving lives because they know that there is no time to lose. When an American athlete is going for gold, he doesn't have a whole lifetime perspective. He does what it takes as soon and as fast as he can. We can go on forever with examples of American efficiency, but we don't have to; it's common knowledge to the world that actions speak louder than words and that Americans are winners when it comes to performing rapidly, rather than using poor words and excuses and getting nothing done.

THE REAL WILD WEST

"**T**HE SHOP OWNER, who was robbed for a fifth time by the same people, knows the names of the criminals and has them on camera." Police dismissed the case because of a lack of evidence.

"*A landlord who was abused by burglars in his own house while his two daughters slept, miraculously managed to catch them. Police did not have the resources to get to the scene of the crime in time for an arrest.*" Later, police dismissed the case because of a lack of evidence.

Headlines like those above are, believe it or not, very common in Norway. We often read about girls who get raped, people who are mugged and victims of blind violence, without any consequences for the criminals. You have to understand that violence and robbery had become virtually absent here in the past, but that has changed drastically the last three decades. What has not changed is the naïve attitude held by politicians and police toward fighting crime. People don't seem to understand that the police should be there to help us out, and to protect us. If I do my best, and think back as long as I can, I can't remember seeing a police officer out in the street. I have to go back many years back to remember my last sighting of a police officer outdoors. We have so many examples of serious and serial criminal actions that do not result in any consequences, even when the police know who the criminals are. And in all this madness, we see victims get arrested after they have protected themselves against cruel criminal actions.

This kind of stupidity doesn't prevent people from getting robbed and raped. Here is one example among many: We thought that the park where the royal castle sits in Norway would be safe for most people, but the fact is that people get robbed there frequently, and women get raped. It's not a big park; if you walk in any direction you will have reached the edge of the park in approximately five minutes. That means it would be pretty easy to catch criminals in the act with only minimal effort from the police. But the police are not even there, so the criminals have nothing to be concerned about. Another example is from three municipalities in Norway. They share one police station, and that station is only open one day per week (Mondays) for just three-and-a-half hours. In Oslo, the capital, most police work during the daytime when criminal activity is significantly less.

We also have very relaxed laws in my country, way too relaxed, if you ask me. It's not unusual to see someone who was sentenced to rape released to the streets a few months later. If you get robbed, and the police catch the guy, you will have the opportunity to meet your robber on the street just minutes later, even though he is a violent, serial thief with many prior convictions. A man who takes another person's life, or even several people's lives, is not locked up for long in Norway. We have many examples of criminals who are coming back on the streets just a few months or a few years after murdering others, whether or not they are considered sane. Where I live, the laws don't work as they should. It's always about pity for the criminals, and it feels like our politicians care more for them than the victims. It's really "The Wild West" over here—the real difference is that in the original Wild West, everyone could protect themselves with weapons, but here, we can't. In Europe, folks normally don't carry weapons; the exception is the criminals who are both illegally armed and very dangerous. That means that it is pretty easy and not much of a risk to be a criminal in my country. The victims are not armed and cannot protect themselves, and the chance of a criminal getting caught is almost absent. If they do get caught, they will not likely get sentenced, but if they do, they will probably be out on the streets very soon, anyway. And, as if that wasn't enough, with all the crime we experience on a daily basis in our country, we have politicians that still have the nerve to say that it is very safe here, and safer here than anywhere else. That's just how it is in Norway.

But there is more! Have you seen the facilities in our jails? Does a private room with your own widescreen TV, refrigerator and shower sound good to you? What about running on the private jogging track, followed by a baking course in the jail's shared kitchen? Other facilities include a recording studio, a fitness room, a library, several types of workshops, a gymnasium and a laboratory. I think you all know by now that to be sentenced to jail in Norway is like a nice, sweet break from everyday life, rather than a punishment that should sting and prevent people from committing crimes again. We actually have people who want to be in jail because of the good facilities. Our pensioners in older homes, who have worked at building our country, live in much worse environments and facilities than the criminals in jail.

People outside of the U.S. have a belief that Americans are very eager to sentence their citizens to jail time. People have an impression that prison time in America is a horrible experience, and that prisons in the U.S. will not have a preventative effect for the people who are eventually released. People think that prisoners who are set free after jail time in the U.S. are far worse individuals than before they went in.

In my opinion, most foreigners have no right to criticize the American justice system; most people don't know much about it, and have little information to lean on. Many have heard stories thru the grapevine that the legal system in America may be corrupt and that misuse of justice happens too frequently. None of the people I have talked to can verify such things, but still, America has a bit of a dilemma because of the specific impressions people have around the world that the legal system in the USA is not to be trusted. I will not and cannot speculate why people have that view, but it exists. People also read statistics about the number of people in jail around the world, and it's verified that the USA has the highest number of people behind bars. In general, most people think there are way too many people behind bars in America and that Americans should do something about it. Many also think that punishments for minor crimes can be too harsh in America. Timothy Jackson has already served sixteen years in a U.S. prison, and will spend the rest of his life in there for stealing a jacket from a department store—set him free, it's a human's life we are talking about here. A similar crime in Norway will not be punished with jail time; he would probably not even get a fine, but that is also wrong, according to people's reactions to justice. I don't have any sympathy for criminals, and especially not for violent criminals, but I can't help to sympathize with Timothy Jackson and similar minor criminals who are spending most of their lives in prison. I think Jackson has paid his dues after sixteen years in prison.

What foreigners do enjoy, more and more, is that they now feel that the USA is a much safer place than before. Foreigners who visited New York or Los Angeles in the past were scared to death, but they now feel much safer there. Even though we, fortunately, still find many places in the world that are quite safe, people seem to appreciate tough and quick responses to violent crimes a lot more now than before. People want safety and justice. They are tired of blind violence that does not suffer any consequences. When it comes to rough crimes, people seem to have more sympathy to the Americans' methods rather than many naïve governments who do nothing to protect their own citizens. I have no doubt that many of the countries in the world could learn from each other on this particular topic, but the overall goal for all countries in the world must be to have peaceful, non-criminal citizens out in the community, instead of behind bars. This also applies to America.

"HAPPY LAND"

"ARE AMERICANS, IN general, happy?"

"If they aren't, they must be the best actors in the world."

That is a typical answer to this question from my interviews. Some people have the impression that Americans fake their happiness, that deep inside they aren't sincere. Many believe that it's nearly impossible to always have such a happy DNA, as Americans seem to have. As a European, I am used to people who look down at the asphalt rather than risk having to make eye contact with another person. I know there is a lot of shyness where I come from, but people in my country don't seem to be happy. Even though we are rated as one of the best and most wealthy countries to live in, I see depressed, introverted people every day; it's terrible to watch and sometimes, it feels like a disease is spread around our country. This also explains how wealth isn't synonymous with happiness—not at all. Money can give a person more freedom to do what he wants with his life, and maybe some moments of joy, like buying a new car, but after that first bliss, money doesn't seem to have much value when it comes to achieving happiness. That is really something to think about for many Americans who dedicate their whole lives to making as much money as possible.

When I visit America, I feel there is something else that is spreading around instead of rude, introverted persons. That something else is laughter, joy, and outgoing people who actually talk to each other. Even if Americans are faking all of that happiness, I'd rather face them than my home citizens. It's much nicer to meet someone who talks openly and looks me in the eye than all the miserable and quiet people we find in my country.

After every trip I've made to America, I miss something when I come home. It's always small, everyday things I think of most, like American politeness. I like when Americans are polite and call me "Sir." In general, it gives people a certain respect and dignity when they are treated as nicely as Americans show toward each other. I miss the liveliness, too. In the USA, there is a charming, noisy energy among people that transmits and gives us extra power. It also gives a sense of being somewhere else, like being on another planet, or in another world somehow. I even miss the talking; nothing is worse than silent people who do not give anything of themselves or who don't show something that explains their thoughts or feelings. Americans are the opposite of that. They may speak nonsense sometimes, but I'd rather listen to that person, which includes eye contact, than talk to a paralyzed person's forehead who never gives me any response. When I'm not in America, I long for the laughter. If you are a sad and unhappy person, there is one good cure for you: Americans. So many have told me that Americans make them happier, even the ones who I know are grumpy by nature loosen up and get happier after spending a while in the U.S. People I have traveled with to the U.S., including myself, have clearly changed into more positive human beings during their stay there. I also love how outgoing Americans are. European students in America are very grateful because Americans have changed them to be much more outgoing, less afraid and, in their own opinion, better at standing out from the crowd. We are talking about students who are so shy that they would rather jump off a bridge than raise their hands in a classroom—extraordinarily introverted, reserved students who are transformed to extroverted, confident people when they step their toes back on the European continent after a stay in the USA. These students now have a superior advantage compared to other students who didn't choose to study in America.

In general, people who feel negatively about America always seem to find something bad to say about the country. But when it comes to being friendly, extroverted and polite, these negative people are often deathly silent, and that is understandable because, for them, it is an inner wish to be honest. The truth is that people in America are generally fine, pleasant and sociable people, but are they really happy?

AMERICAN POP CULTURE

PEOPLE AROUND THE world are well-acquainted with many American actors and musicians. They have had a close relationship to these artists and have followed them for many years. They buy anything that is related to these artists, and many worship them enormously.

Americans seem to always create commercial entertainment that is tempting for the mass market in most parts of the world. Americans were pioneers in the field and are still world leaders when it comes to providing good entertainment the whole human race can enjoy. Yet, we see other countries that deliver great artistic talents, like people from the United Kingdom, France and Australia. These artists will often also end up in American show business somehow, whether in a role in a movie, signing a deal with an American record label or something else. To get an opportunity like that will take them straight to the world market, instead of limiting them to their own country. Americans understand that making a great song, a good movie or a funny or exciting theater performance only gets you halfway to success. Americans have the know-how about marketing and how to use channels and distribution to make a specific project successful in many parts of the world, instead of limiting themselves to sales only in the U.S.

With that said, there is also a change in other places in the world. They have become more professional in many other countries, and Americans must be prepared for greater competition in commercial entertainment and world entertainment distribution from continents such as Asia, as well as parts of Europe.

One problem for Americans is that youngsters in the world feel that a lot of American pop and hip-hop music has turned too weird to understand and impossible to relate with. People seem to enjoy world music more now; they like sincere musicians and many are saying straight out that they don't like all the "clowns" that abound in the American pop music industry that can neither sing nor dance. It's important to know that people who are saying these things are not negative about American culture and music from the beginning; in fact, many of them are quite the opposite, and have been very fond of American music and entertainers for many years, but they really don't like recent developments in the American entertainment industry. Many think the American music industry has turned really weird with strange music and stupid lyrics. They feel that it no longer matters if you have a good song or are a great singer because the industry is dishonest and superficial. They miss quality entertainment and actually feel pity for Americans who have to hear and see all the terrible musical entertainment that U.S. musicians are popping out regularly. It shouldn't be a big surprise for America to know that the cultural elite people of the world find American pop culture to be shallow, but what is more surprising is that the non-elite population feels the same way. They actually find themselves lucky to not have Americans' pop-culture music in their life on a daily basis. People are telling me that they enjoy local artists and music more than before, music that they both understand and feel is more sincere. But it is not all grim, there is one genre in the American music industry that people like very well, and that is actually country music. I say "actually" because that genre is something you don't hear often on radio stations around the world. But there is this a general opinion that country musicians write genuine songs, have thoughtful, sincere lyrics and that their songwriting is incredibly skilled. Other well-liked genres are jazz, Latino music, singer/ songwriter and old-style crooner music. New American rock music artists have also turned too strange in people's minds, but not as strange as hip-hoppers and pop artists. However, always remember that these opinions do not apply to all artists in America—it's rather a general impression.

There is also global competition in the movie business, nowadays. Countries like India and China are making an effort to be distributed globally, but to say that these movies are blockbusters outside their own country isn't exactly true. But still, we should keep an eye on them as movie reviewers around the world are often fond of their films. European countries like Great Britain, Italy, Denmark and France have, for many years, produced gold in film, and they seem to have achieved an even wider audience outside of their own countries in the last few years. British broadcaster BBC is still producing pearls on a string in the film and television industry. Downton Abbey, Harry Potter and James Bond are all results of wonderful creativity from British writers, producers, directors, actors and many other cultural workers. Also, in moviemaking, people find American film productions to be shallower than that of other countries, and many would like American films to be more serious. Personally, I think American films are diverse and I like to be entertained in a movie. But, I identify with what these people mean, and know that many haven't seen the serious side of the American film industry. It seems that the American pop culture films have a much wider reach than the more serious and artistic films.

But entertainment is more than movies and modern music; it includes dancers, sportsmen, magicians, comedians and many other hard skilled workers. It's fair to say that the general impression from the outside is that Americans are very professional in all these areas in the entertainment industry, but it's also fair to say that Americans must keep their focus on serious quality cultural work, in addition, to continue their reputation as great producers of important entertainment. On the other hand, the American entertainment industry is still very tempting for many cultural workers in the world, and somehow America seems to continue to be attractive for such artists.

American pop culture is well-known in most parts of the world. In Europe, we find countries that actually seem more American than America itself, such as the Scandinavian countries. At least, that's what Americans themselves are saying when they visit these countries. They can't believe what they are experiencing: burger bars, American music, Coca-Cola, movies, American steak houses and American brands displayed on stores and clothes almost everywhere. It's not unusual to hear Aerosmith played in a tropical bar on a desert island in the Indian Ocean, or to find a kid wearing Nike shoes in a remote town in Russia. To visit a small Italian village and meet a boy wearing a Michael Jordan t-shirt is also pretty normal these days. Many of the citizens of the world are acquainted with American media, people and brands like: Superman, Elvis, Madonna, the New York Yankees, the L.A. Lakers, the Dallas Cowboys, John Wayne, E.T., André Agassi, Nike, McDonalds, Muhammad Ali and many, many more. This is both good and bad. We have already been through the problems people are facing through junk food and Western diseases. People get sick from well-known American foods, like McDonalds, but that's only one side of it. The other side is that the local food producers don't have as many customers as they need to survive. The huge factories in China and other places, especially in Asia, produce American pop-culture food products for almost zero cost, and the factory owners of places like that will, because of the low pricing and high competition, pay their workers only the bare minimum.

Around the world, people are also afraid of losing their own traditions and culture in exchange for American pop culture. Take Halloween, for example, a holiday that not many people had even heard of here in Norway two decades ago. Now, everyone is celebrating it, but they don't know why they celebrate it. Our Christmas celebration is also very American, incorporating the American Santa Claus and Disney films.

I guess you all now understand that American pop culture has infected many parts of the world, and, in general, people seem to like a lot of things that can be related to America. The exception is when there is something they don't understand that threatens their business, culture or existence, or when something does not appear sincere enough to them.

The mantra for American pop-culture and show-business producers, who still want to reach out to the whole world, must therefore be: Make top quality entertainment, and change it so it is both believable and consumable for the whole world, not only for Americans.

OLD AMERICA

WHEN PEOPLE SAY to me that they like America, their statement is often synonymous with what they liked about America from the past. People, all around the world, have a huge admiration for America as it was in the 1950s and 60s, but other time periods also stand out in noteworthy ways, especially for all the immigrants who came to America. So, during my travels, and in order to write this book, I actually had to specify to people that this book is about America as it is today and not a sentimental "travel-back-in-time" thing. But let us travel back anyway for a little while so we can summarize what people did say about America as it was before, and maybe today's America can benefit from that time too.

First of all, there is no doubt that both Americans and foreigners loved America when a car looked like a car. Everybody misses old American classic cars; it was not the power of the engine in these cars, or the size of them that mattered, it was the feeling people got from the incredible driving experience. Many had their own favorite model and treated their cars better than their girlfriends. To drive an old classic car is to give a sense of liberty and an impression of being a part of the American dream. But it isn't only the old cars that are missed, it's the American lifestyle offered during these years that had such an impact on the world population that many people are still living like that today—men who still wear old, classic leather jackets, with their hair full of grease and women in old, classic dresses, who come together for gatherings that include all the ingredients from that time, like old rock music, burgers, classic furniture, pictures featuring mid-century brands and old movie posters. They just don't want to let go of that lifestyle that they think is the best that ever was. But, if you believe that it is just the nursing home generation of today who had such an attraction for that lifestyle, think again. At least half of the people I have talked to who had such thoughts have been under thirty years old; they weren't even alive during their heralded period of time, but they still dare to walk around dressed up like Elvis or Marilyn Monroe. What I have discovered in these interviews is that the old, classic American lifestyle had no borders or age limitations. It fit right in to every household in the world—man or woman, son or daughter, Europe, Asia or the USA—it didn't really matter, it's still, in the twenty-first century, one of the strongest brandings alive.

People from all over the world have been very eager to explain why America was better as it was in the past, and there are always three good reasons that stand out from that time period, and probably will stand out in the future, as the best of America. They are: quality, originality and honesty.

The people back in the "old America" were understandable and seemed similar to the rest of us. We could relate and identify with them and we all dreamed about their lifestyle. Today, where even the kids don't understand American pop culture, America has moved further away from a world that hasn't gone in the same direction. People say that America no longer has its own identity. Many can't even name any positive keywords to describe America as it is today, but they can easily come up with negative words;

Greedy, fat, unintelligent, broke and superficial are only some of them.

Today, if we look at the products that were made from that "old America" time period, we could immediately say it comes from that period of time. No other currently-available products have such special and standout design and quality. These quality-made items cost more to make, but are also more appreciated. People don't want cheap products if the quality is poor. Around the world, I can still see old American stuff from the 50s that works well and looks as new as if it was bought yesterday—quality resistant, everlasting products that never seem to be destroyed. Listen to the songs from that time: timeless music, with sincere lyrics, that has been admired by the world for all these years, and yet still is admired today. The keywords quality, originality and honesty unfortunately seem not to be in focus in today's America, and that is something that people miss about America. So to have these keywords in mind, in addition to thinking about how people still feel about old American products, could be a very clear hint for any new developer and manufacturer in the U.S. They also may be the keywords for a new, up-and-coming, successful manufacturing age in America.

YOUNG AMERICANS

AMERICANS HAVE CHANGED in recent years and, sadly, people say that it's not a change for the better. Many found most Americans to be very admirable, kind and understandable back in the old days, but now they find more negative skepticism, sometimes beyond their understanding. The universal feeling is that youngsters in old America could conduct themselves appropriately in the past, but that isn't how things are nowadays. Before, it didn't seem to matter what rank of society the American came from, people could meet any American around the world or in the U.S. and communicate with that person politely.

Today, many young people in this world don't understand the American youth. They say that the youngsters in America have changed for the worse in terms of being disinterested in many things in life, that the youngsters today have an unenthusiastic attitude toward life and a negative vision about their own futures. People also have the impression that the behavior of young Americans is abnormal; they suspect that young Americans are taking too many drugs and that they have turned into more erratic and less attractive people to be around. People are also concerned about the future mental health of America. I don't know if there is a big debate about this topic in the U.S., but if it isn't, people outside think it should be. It's not positive that America now generates youth that seem to be negative, non-communicative and intimidating to the rest of the world—kids that appear to be in different worlds than the rest of us. I won't speculate why so many young ones have turned unpleasant in the U.S., but it is definitely not a development that America should hide under a bed. These kids are, in fact, the future of America. I have personally seen negative changes among youth, not only in America, but especially there. So, if I'm in a place to give any advice at all on this, I suggest including the young ones of the American society more and as soon as possible. Give them responsibilities, preferably right after their high school years or even while they're still in high school. The fact that many youngsters don't have a future to aim for or to believe in is destroying those that are insecure from the beginning their lives. In fact, it's understandable that youngsters turn their back to a society that does not offer them something they want. Give them freedom to choose, but at the same time have high demands on them. Youngsters want, as do the rest of us, to be happy, active and to do things they like. Everyone must have the real opportunity to do something they enjoy, even if they are busy at school or at work. Give them that happiness! The young ones must also get out of the house to be more active; don't let them sit inside and play videogames by themselves every day, as that is not a good approach for a meaningful, healthy life. Teach them from an early age to be in tune with nature; it's good medicine for both mind and body. And have rules for them. The young ones I know actually want rules; they want clear limits for what they can or cannot do, so don't forget to create boundaries and make sure that these rules are followed. You will be thanked later. When I visit Great Britain especially, but also countries like Greece and Thailand, I meet so many nice, young, fine, polite teenagers who are so well-behaved. They are wonderful, happy youngsters with high goals for the future. The kids in these countries have had regular, clear and understandable rules to follow. They are also kept away from drugs.

But we elders must also understand that the world has changed, in some ways for worse, but, actually, in a lot of ways for the better. We must also understand that America, and this whole world, will not be like it was before, even if we wanted it to be. The fact is that adults must adjust to the world as we see it now, rather than dreaming of the past and wishing for the old America back. The "new America" is here for good, and the "future America" will be even more different than today's America, and that is something we all will be a part of. Kids today understand this and have understood it for a long time, whereas many elder Americans still don't seem to realize it. This alone may be one good reason why many people in the world are noticing these huge differences and for the lack of understanding between the younger and older generations in America.

We must recognize that to involve and help the youngsters in America reach for a better, more meaningful life is also a way to help ourselves, as well as our generation's future. We must admit that young people are our future, and that it's every adult's responsibility to guide them through their journey to their adult lives.

We must let every human being in the USA have their basic needs met to stay mentally healthy—let people contribute and feel significant. Show your affection and love for your friends, partner, sons and daughters. Let the youngsters be important to others. If they get the feeling that they are important in someone else's life, they will feel valuable and recognized. Youngsters need to have contentment in their life, not riches in their wallets.

The way I see it, America can certainly achieve a long and bright future if they bother to help the young generation move in the right direction. But, since the world is constantly changing, it will be a new and different direction than before, a future that engages everyone, and especially the youth. The reality is pretty clear to me: if you don't include the young ones and have them on your side, there could, in fact, be dark clouds in the horizon for the future of America.

ATTRACTIVE, UNATTRACTIVE AMERICANS

MANY FOREIGNERS THINK that Americans either look like attractive, skinny movie stars or overweight, unattractive eating machines, and there is nothing in between—the average-built American doesn't exist. In fact, people who have never been in the U.S. before think that everybody looks like beauty queens and kings, while the ones who have been in the U.S. have the stereotypical opinion that there is only either great-looking or very fat people that exist there.

But why do people have such a superficial impression of many Americans? Here are my reflections about it: Most people who visit the USA are visiting the most popular states, like California, Nevada, Florida and New York, mostly because of the warm weather, but also for other reasons like their nearness to the sea, scenery and entertainment found in Orlando, Las Vegas or San Francisco. Such places attract people from all over the world, but they also attract citizens from all over America. Many people who move to such states are people from the entertainment industry and people with dreams to fulfill. Many of the world's athletes live and practice their sports in California and Florida, partly because of the climate, but also because the most elite coaches and competitors live there, too. Their management is also often there, and it's the place for sponsors and basically where the money is. Athletes who want to be the best in the world have to be where they can have all of these things mentioned above nearby, in addition to the best training conditions and equal competition. There are usually just a few places in the world where you get all of these factors at the same time, and, often, we find all these things in certain states in America.

For a theatre actress, her ultimate dream is to one day be on a Broadway stage. She would do anything to achieve that dream including moving to New York and attending Broadway auditions. Stock traders and many other businessmen, especially in real estate, find that Wall Street in New York City is the place to be. Los Angeles is world-famous for their movie and music industries, so actors and directors, as well as stuntmen and music producers, all with high ambitions, move to LA to get the dream job they have been longing for. For a magician, his own Las Vegas show is the ultimate goal, and he must live there to achieve his dream. Personally, I've never seen more beautiful girls at once than I have seen in Las Vegas, Nevada but many of these girls aren't even from Nevada. They come from all over America and even from many other places in the world. Attractive girls move to Las Vegas for work and fortune, and Vegas is always searching for pretty girls. In short, the USA attracts students, professionals, well-educated and trained people from all over the world, and some states get more migrants because of the position they are in, what they have to offer and their history. For example, Houston attracts people for their oil and spaceflight industries.

When I was an active barefoot water-skier, my Norwegian national water-skiing team went to Winter Haven every winter, a tiny town in Florida between Tampa and Orlando, close to Cypress Gardens. It was a very small town with not much going on. So, why would we be stupid enough to even think about traveling so far to such a place? It was for several reasons. First of all, we could escape the Norwegian winter to have summer and warm water, although all the lakes were full of alligators. Also, we were trained by world champions from both Australia and the USA, and there were compatible athletes there, like the American world champion. There were also people we could network with. And lastly, we had great, world-class entertainment within a close driving distance.

When I decided to record my first demo tape as a songwriter, I was searching the Internet to find a great producer for the job. After months of research I realized that the USA was the only place to go—it was there that I could work with top people in the industry. Where else in the world could I have the opportunity to work with a producer who has also worked with Alicia Keys, Santana, Missy Elliot, Madonna and Will Smith, among many others? As a bonus, the recording studio was located in the center of Times Square in Manhattan, New York (also known as New York City), with all the benefits that city has to offer.

My point is that some specific states in the U.S. attract certain, often attractive, people from the whole world. Miami, Florida, has always been one of the favored locations for supermodels and photographers in the fashion industry, while Hawaii attracts surfers and sunbathers. Such warm locations, cities and states, with many hours of sunlight and a lot of things going on, attract foreign tourists who probably would come home with a very different impression of America than if they visited a less tourist-friendly "fly-over state" than states like New York or California. In fact, New York, Florida, California and similar states have a diverse international population at all times and are, therefore, not comparable with other "real" American states that appear to be more native.

AN AMERICAN IS NOT REALLY A
STEREOTYPICAL AMERICAN

S
OME FOLKS MAY think that I have written too many
positive views about America in this book, but if you read
this book carefully you saw that Americans got a good dose
of both positive and negative feedback. In my interview sessions, I
tried to use really significant, critical questions, but to be honest, I
thought that the USA would come out looking worse out than it
did. Many have told me that the USA is synonymous with auto-
matic negative connotations, and that tells me that people have
expressed way too many undeserved falsehoods about America over
the last few decades. But this book proves many critics wrong, and
those who easily throw out negative statements about the USA will
probably be less likely to do so in the future after having read this
book. Most Americans don't live up to the stereotypical American
profile, and a problem that America has had for many years, and
will probably face in the future, is that people spread quick-witted
negative statements they have heard from others about the country.
It seems that people have pre-determined opinions and statements
to tell me when I ask them a question about America, and that is
why I have emphasized that people must share their own true opinions during our conversations. I let people think for themselves
for a moment before they answered, and then asked them once
again what they really meant. Sometimes I had to go back to them
and ask them further questions to fully understand what they were
trying to say, so I trust that we have more accurate results than
ever before of what people sincerely think about Americans. People

don't think any one American is identical to a fellow American; people know that each American is different and that there are as many positive and negative aspects about the USA as there are in every other country in the world. People also understand that there is a big difference between the views of American politicians and those of the average person who lives there. It shouldn't surprise anyone that people who live in America have their own diverse thoughts on the problems within their country, as well as on foreign issues, but sometimes it does cause surprise. There will always be people who willingly say untrue statements about America because some people actually believe that all Americans are the same, but even worse, many people express negative things about the USA without knowing the country or without having their own sincere opinions. They just say what's popular to say whether or not they are wrong or right. I even know people who speak against their own beliefs just to fit in to a crowd or to avoid conflicts or discussions. There will always be people who repeat what others have told them, as if it were their own opinion, without any consideration for if there is a grain of real truth in it. People like that are actually giving Americans a hard time and a terrible reputation, and creating falsehoods. But, as mentioned before, we all have positive and negative issues to deal with in every country in the world, and there is really no point to sweep that under the rug. Where do we really find a perfect country? Russia? China? Germany? Norway? If we compare the USA to many other countries in western civilization or the world, I don't see Americans come across as any worse than others. On some subjects Americans win, and on some they lose. For example, where do we find the friendliest people in the world? Many will often immediately say America. I wrote a similar book about Norway and the Norwegians came out as rude, non-friendly and introverted people. That was, of course, a surprise to many of my fellow citizens who think very highly of themselves. Rudeness is generally not an issue Americans need to deal with; they are polite, right and true, and people around the world know that and seem to appreciate them. When it comes to innovation, the whole world is grateful to America for giving them all the products made by Americans.

America is still a country many people dream to be a part of and most people understand the diversity this country has to offer. They know that any one American isn't like any other American; Each American has different beliefs with diverse skills and lifestyles.

THE DEAD AMERICAN COUNTRYSIDE

I N AMERICA, WE now find a vast number of small ghost towns and surrendered farms. We find whole communities that have moved out, empty buildings, empty gas stations, old wrecks of classic cars and rusty tractors; we also find schools and churches that are abandoned. Some buildings have been taken over by drug dealers, criminals or homeless people. All of these surrendered places provide memories of a wonderful period of time for the American people, and my heart bleeds every time I see these buildings empty and abandoned. So I wonder, is it no longer possible for people in America to live in small towns or rural areas anymore? I think it is. I will not make any conclusions about why people have moved away from the places they once cared about and wanted to live in, but I believe it all comes down to the economy, and the possibility of a future in these specific areas. The American government should make it attractive for people to live in the whole country, including the countryside, and there are several instruments to achieve such effect on people. These techniques include lower taxes for the farmers who grow sustainable and organic food, financial support for new factories who dare to innovate, inexpensive properties for everyone, good schools, strong infrastructure and cultural facilities, but most of all, it must be trendy to live and work outside of the cities. It's also probably healthier for the American population if people find jobs all throughout America. It will provide not only steady work, but also pride and such positive actions will also cause possible spillovers for all of America through less crime, less unemployment and, therefore, less cost and more income for the American government. It will, in general, give a positive vibe to all of America and is a win-win situation. It's not about moving all of the American population to the countryside, it's about giving people who want to live there a chance to have a decent life. It's also about helping America not lose their middle class because that will not benefit anyone—not even the wealthiest one percent of America that owns most of the country. It's not good to have only poor and rich people in a country; that will give every business owner fewer customers and result in too many poor people, without a hope for the future, and will generate a country full of illegal activities. Therefore, I can't see any other solution than to create jobs that last, let communities grow and create life and opportunities all over America—in the cities, but especially in the countryside. This could be the best investment Americans could do for themselves, and something that will make the American people feel even more pride, as they should.

CARPE DIEM

THE LATIN WORDS "Carpe diem" mean "Seize the day". I believe that many people around the world are abusing this phrase. People, in general, are saying it too easily without thinking about the real meaning of it. It's like people are trying to convince themselves that they feel better than they actually do and it's sad that the idea of a way of living becomes more important than living the actual life. But, what I have learned during this journey is that, for Americans, these words mean more. Countless people I have talked to say that Americans are synonymous with "turning words into actions," that Americans really do what they say they will do. Unfortunately, that is not the case for all Americans anymore. Something has changed.

I once met a man who used this Latin cliché frequently. He urged others to "Carpe diem!"; he told people to live their lives to the fullest! But who gave him the right to lecture others when his life was quite vacuous? How could he, who had no life himself, guide others to achieve the perfect life?

Talking to that man gave me a wakeup call, so I will use the same cliché, one more time, just to come to an end point of this book.

Carpe Diem. Let me be really honest now. Have I really taken hold of every day as I should? Many people haven't always seized the day, either. But is that a good excuse for me to only exist without feeling alive? Perhaps I once thought that I lived as I wanted to, but I now understand that I was lying to myself while saying such stupid things as, "Now my life is good" and "I'm living like it is the last day of my life." To be completely honest it was a joke and a lie every time these thoughts came to my mind. So after days, weeks and years with self-examination, I finally understand that my life is nothing to be proud of. I existed; I went to work and paid my bills, but I never listened to my true, inner wishes. I never went after what was important to me. I had no progress in life. I always thought about the days in the past that were lost, and the days in the future that should become so much better, without doing anything to make these future days any brighter. I never appreciated the present day. Maybe I wasn't as brave and outgoing as I thought I was. Please don't misunderstand me, I was okay and I didn't see any reason to change my life drastically. I was safe, I had a good salary and the cave back home was very comfortable while lying in bed in front of the TV screen. There was no one who contradicted me, nor anyone who required or expected something more from me. In my mind and in my own little truth, I was kind of happy, and it was very leisurely and calm. But to address the question, "Did I live my own life?" No, never—I didn't even live for a second in that time period, and that is the ugly truth. I would say it so strongly that I approached the abyss, because these feelings of comfortableness gave me a feeling of uncomfortableness. To have nothing meaningful to do, to have nothing to fight for, nothing to dread or look forward to, and no one to take account of made me emotionally numb. I had become the "living dead."

"You cannot find peace by avoiding life."

Virginia Woolf, English writer

To not take any risks in life is the largest game of chance you can play. To not take actions in your life will guarantee an end to your hope for a better life. To not take actions can include not facing jealousy, not meeting new people you might dislike, avoiding uncomfortable situations, avoiding facing problems at work or in your social life. Comfortable? Yes, but you will have both legs planted safely in the coffin. If you don't want to go out that door, you will never experience the meaning of your life or any kind of love for that matter. Without affection and passion for a job, a hobby, nature, a girlfriend or boyfriend or for life itself, it would all be meaningless. Every human being should feel such love for something and by participating in your own life and really listening to what you essentially must have—to listen to what you are craving—only then will you become yourself and feel truly alive and present. Be available for people around you. Be completely honest about the life you want to live. Turn that TV off and get out of your house as soon as possible. Live now. Go from words to actions; be a doer and an achiever, not only a dreamer. Dare to find your own path, because if you do, the most wonderful thing in life can and will happen to you. Some Americans already understand this and, as a result, they are living extraordinary lives. But many, especially young Americans, must now learn to find their path, and they will most likely learn it from their elders because there has been a drastic change in the modern America, a change that is keeping many people away from daily social life and employment. These people must be included somehow; they must feel that they are needed. That is something every business owner and every leader across America must take on and understand. Include everyone; it's human, it's vital and it's absolute necessary for keeping a mentally-healthy America. A human being needs to feel development. Give people a chance to have progress in life, and then you will raise winners.

So, if you are that person who hasn't found yourself quite yet, don't wait anymore. Do not abandon yourself, go out and live your life. Your dreams can come true, not only in America, but especially in America. It doesn't matter what you are aiming for because the most important thing is that you are doing it; the road itself is the answer to happiness. If you are honest and feel that what you are doing is essential, then it's the right direction for you. The journey itself, being part of something bigger, part of the world—there is actually no other way to live, and it's a wonderful feeling to know that your life is going forward and not standing still or even going backward.

"Your own journey toward your goals will itself create happiness."

Rene Zografos

I have now sworn that I must live my life, as I want it to be, to not lose more time or listen to others who are saying everything is impossible. I understand now that to make myself happy is actually the same as making people around me happy. So, I made the promise to myself to chase my dreams and passions and to fulfill them. Since that promise, I've been happier than ever. Even though I sometimes face resistance and battles, I feel better. I'm doing all these impossible things that others said I couldn't do. Since I started to make these promises to myself and, more importantly, put them into actions every day, I have achieved more in just a few years than in my whole life before, and good things just seem to come by themselves now. But, I still have new, and in many other people's opinions, impossible dreams and tasks to fulfill. Well, I have already proven these critics wrong and I will gladly do it again, because as long as I follow my passion, I am living my dream—my American dream—and the only voice I need to listen to is my own—to what I need deep down inside. Thanks to the process and journey of writing this book, I now also feel different and more open, a better human being, almost invincible and more American, somehow. I have accomplished writing a book in a foreign language. It took me many years with small steps every day, and I made it through the storm, as I have done before. As a consequence of writing this book, it has resulted in priceless meetings with wonderful people and cultures. A true gift was given to me: I achieved happiness. So I know now, even more certainly than ever before, that good things can happen if I follow my path, as long as I throw myself into it with all my power. Success or failure doesn't really seem to matter anymore because the kind of success I want is already here, right now, while I'm pursuing my new goals and ambitions! The answer to success and happiness is, in fact, not money, not bigger houses or any other wealth. The answer is easier than that; it's honesty. It's honesty to choose the direction your inner voice tells you to and to follow the road of the life you want to live, and that is, for sure, a hell of a better ride than the alternative.

You can do it, everyone can. Be true and honest about what you are burning for in your life and go for it, with all your strength, every day. Go out and enjoy the holy life you are given. Right now is your time on this earth, so be sincere, be brave, be loved, be admired—be a genuine American, and Carpe Diem.

Sources: Yearbook of American and Canadian Churches, Statistical Abstract of the United States, USA.gov, U.S Census Bureau, Internetworldstats, cityblock, america.gov, Hello magazine, Google, New York Observer, Stella magazine, NRK, CBS news, Mark Huffman, Wikipedia, Huffington Post, The American Institute of Stress, TV2, TV3, Deloitte Center for Financial Services, Dagens Naringsliv, Bureau of Justice and Statistics, Save the Children, BI, Legatum Prosperity Index, mindully.org, Finansavisen, Bloomberg, Forbes, The Wall Street Journal, The Atlantic, Tradelogy, PEW Research Center, people around the world